Balancing the Books

CERC Monograph Series No.4

Balancing the Books

Household Financing of Basic Education in Cambodia

Mark Bray
Seng Bunly

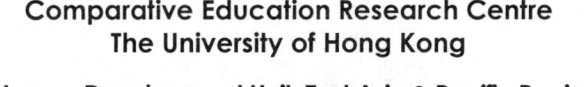

Comparative Education Research Centre
The University of Hong Kong

Human Development Unit, East Asia & Pacific Region
The World Bank

First published 2005
Comparative Education Research Centre
Faculty of Education
The University of Hong Kong
Pokfulam Road, Hong Kong, China

In collaboration with the Human Development Unit, East Asia & Pacific Region,
The World Bank

© Comparative Education Research Centre

ISBN 962 8093 39 8

Cover design: Vincent Lee

Cover photograph: UNESCO, reproduced with permission

Layout: Annie Lai

Contents

List of Abbreviations and Acronyms

ADB	Asian Development Bank
CCLS	Cambodia Child Labour Survey
COMPASS	COMmunity and PArents in Support of Schools
CSES	Cambodia Socio-Economic Survey
EFA	Education for All
ESSP	Education Sector Support Program
EQIP	Education Quality Improvement Project
FPE	Free Primary Education
GDP	Gross Domestic Product
HIV/AIDS	Human Immunodeficiency Virus/Acquired Immune Deficiency Syndrome
JFPR	Japan Fund for Poverty Reduction
KAPE	Kampuchean Action for Primary Education
MoEYS	Ministry of Education, Youth & Sport
NGO	Non-Governmental Organisation
OECD	Organisation for Economic Co-operation & Development
PAP	Priority Action Programme
PRGF	Poverty Reduction and Growth Facility
PTA	Parent-Teacher Association
UNDP	United Nations Development Programme
UNESCO	United Nations Educational, Scientific & Cultural Organization
UNICEF	United Nations Children's Fund
UPE	Universal Primary Education
US	United States
WCEFA	World Conference on Education for All
WEF	World Education Forum
WFP	World Food Programme

Exchange Rates

Between 1998 and the time of writing this book, the exchange rate between the US dollar and the Cambodian riel was stable at approximately US$1 = 4,000 riels. The US dollar itself circulates widely in Cambodia, particularly in urban areas. Prior to 1998 the Cambodian currency suffered from rapid inflation, and at that time US dollars were widely felt to provide more stability.

List of Tables

List of Figures

Acknowledgements

Many people have assisted in the production of this study. Some can be mentioned by name, but others remain anonymous, in part because they are members of large groups. First to be acknowledged are the many people who provided data, especially those in schools and communities. These are among the people who cannot be mentioned by name because they are so numerous. Nevertheless, the authors thank them for their willingness to share information and for their courtesy and assistance at every stage.

Also to be acknowledged are specific individuals who guided the study, who provided information, and who commented on drafts. In the World Bank, Luis Benveniste initiated the task and together with Cristóbal Ridao-Cano provided valuable advice. Vin McNamara was an invaluable informant and guide at all stages, and the authors greatly appreciate his willingness to share his wisdom and many years of experience. In the data collection, data processing and dissemination workshops, particular thanks must be given Hov Levin and the other staff of BN Consult. Finally, the authors thank the additional individuals who made most helpful comments on drafts, and particularly Luise Ahrens, Lynn Dudley, Richard Geeves, Sopheak Keng, Elizabeth King, Mitsuko Maeda and Anthony Sweeting.

Cambodia
Provincial Boundaries

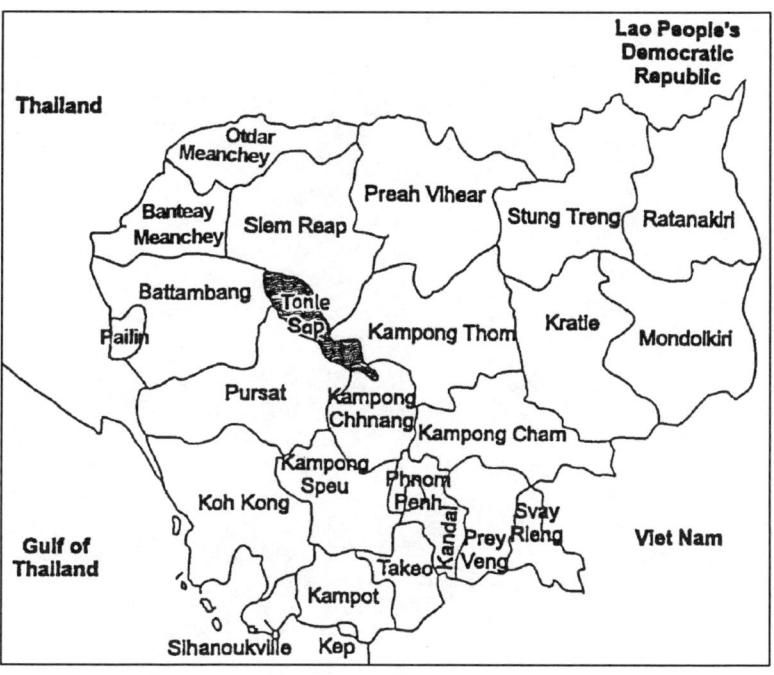

Introduction

Across the world, provision of basic education is widely viewed as primarily a government responsibility. Education is seen as a human right, and governments are expected to resource public systems of education to serve their peoples. Private schools may exist in parallel to public ones, but they are usually seen as supplementary to the public systems of education, serving families who desire superior quality and/or schooling with particular religious or other special orientations.

Accompanying these perceptions about the role of governments and about education as a human right are the notions that all children should go to school to receive a basic education of appropriate quantity and quality, and that schooling in public systems of education should be free of charge. Powerful economic and social arguments can be advanced to support these notions. However, advocacy can sometimes become simplistic. Advocates sometimes ignore the fact that schooling always has to be paid for by somebody, and that, especially in low-income countries, many governments lack the resources needed to achieve universal education of even the lowest quality. Further, when goods and services are distributed totally free of charge, they are commonly under-valued by the recipients. In some settings, it may be asserted, consumers should at least be permitted and perhaps should be asked to contribute to the costs of schooling. While some members of the public have low incomes and cannot easily afford to pay for schooling, other groups have middle or high incomes and can afford such payments. Financial contributions might not only encourage the consumers to value the services more highly, but would also reduce the demands on government resources and could thus allow more and better services to be provided to low income groups.

A further notion to enter the debate concerns the full costs of education. Economists commonly distinguish between the direct and indirect costs of schooling. Direct costs include those which are met by providers of schooling plus the additional costs which are met by households for uniforms, books, transport and related items. Indirect costs include the opportunity costs of income foregone when pupils attend school rather than engaging in other activities. The indirect costs are a major burden for some households, particularly the poorest, and can be a significant determinant of whether or not a child attends school. Some families, explicitly or implicitly, conduct informal cost-benefit analyses on whether or not it is useful to send children to school. Of course many cultural and other factors also shape decisions on school attendance; but one factor is the question whether the economic benefits are likely to outweigh the total package of direct and indirect costs to households.

These considerations underlie the main title of this book. The term "balancing the books" is most commonly used in accounting to refer to the need for expenditures to match incomes. When expenditures are higher than incomes, then the books are not balanced. The books are also unbalanced when incomes are higher than expenditures, though this situation is usually less problematic. One major task for governments is to ensure that education systems can be financed, i.e. that sufficient revenues exist to cover at least the direct costs of those education systems. Revenues can of course come from many sources, of which the most important in the majority of countries is domestic taxation. Low income countries may also receive external aid in the form of grants and loans. Yet after addition of all the revenues, a gap may still exist between the costs of schooling and the resources available to governments. In such cases, household contributions may be necessary simply to balance the books.

Some governments in such circumstances allow patterns to develop by default. The authorities provide what resources they can, and then leave the consumers to find ways to bridge gaps as best they can. While such default arrangements may be workable, they are usually undesirable. It is preferable for governments first to calculate clearly what they are able to provide, and then to work out who will have to bridge what gaps and with what consequences. Deliberate policies of this type can help ensure that burdens do not fall unduly on the poor. Arrangements can be made for resources to be contributed by middle-income and prosperous groups, and further arrangements can be made to alleviate the burdens on the poorest. Thus the accountants' books can be balanced in different ways according to specific strategies devised by policy makers.

The metaphor about balancing the books can be stretched a little further to cover other dimensions in decision-making. When households undertake informal cost-benefit analyses to decide whether or not to send their children to school, they are in effect balancing other priorities against books (or book-learning, education). Left to themselves, households may decide that the balance of costs and benefits favours other priorities rather than books. However, governments which feel that schooling is of great importance not only to individuals but to whole societies may decide to intervene by adjusting the weights in the balance. Thus in some circumstances governments may feel that schooling does not have to be completely free of charge, and that at least some households can and should provide resources to education through direct channels (as opposed to indirect channels such as taxation). Alternatively, governments may decide that no charges will be levied for schooling itself, but that households will remain responsible for items such as uniforms and transportation, and for supplementary tutoring if they desire it. In a further option, governments may endeavour to meet these extra costs for at least some households, in effect providing scholarships to cover all visible costs of schooling. And in a yet further option, governments may endeavour to influence the cost-benefit analyses by meeting even the opportunity costs of schooling, providing subsidies to encourage children to go to school rather than engage in other activities.

In this book, the above issues are discussed first in general and then with specific reference to Cambodia. Household costs of schooling arise in all settings, but have been especially prominent in Cambodia because successive governments have found themselves short of resources and unable to meet all needs. The Cambodian deficit has been more extreme than in most other countries, but has been the focus of far-reaching policy reforms which have had an impressive impact. While the book will have a strong audience in Cambodia itself, it also has a relevance to policy makers elsewhere who face resource constraints and who are considering measures to address balances in the financing of education.

The book is a sequel to a publication written by Bray (1999a) and entitled *The Private Costs of Public Schooling: Household and Community Financing of Primary Education in Cambodia*. That book showed (p.42) that in the late 1990s households and communities in Cambodia were meeting an estimated 59.0 per cent of the total resources for primary schooling, even in the public system of education.

The government was providing an estimated 12.5 per cent, politicians through various channels provided an estimated 10.4 per cent, and non-governmental organisations (NGOs) and external agencies provided an estimated 18.0 per cent. The remaining 0.1 per cent came from other school-generated income. In international terms the proportion of costs met by households was very large, and Cambodia could therefore be considered a special case deserving attention from a comparative perspective.

The present work builds on the 1999 book in two ways. First it updates analysis in the primary school sector, presenting information on changes over time. It does this by examining precisely the same sample of schools and their communities, which were selected from locations around the country. Second, the book supplements data on primary schooling with data on lower secondary schooling, which permits identification of the increasing burdens on households at higher levels of the system. The title of the book refers to basic education. In Cambodia, as elsewhere, basic education is an umbrella term which encompasses primary plus lower secondary education. Primary education in Cambodia has a standard duration of six years, though some children may repeat classes and others may drop out before the end, and lower secondary education has a standard duration of three years.

The 1999 book arose from work commissioned by UNESCO and by UNICEF in conjunction with the Ministry of Education, Youth & Sport (MoEYS) in Cambodia. It was mainly based on a survey of the household and community costs of education in 1997/98, and its data and analysis became an important input to education reforms in Cambodia (see e.g. Kemmerer 1999, pp.12-17; National EFA Assessment Group 1999, p.12; MoEYS & KAPE 2001, p.12). The book was also welcomed by the international community, which recognised that the topic was of considerable importance and that few countries had data of the type presented. Brock (2001, p.249), for example, noted that the study provided "rich insights into the real problems of education financing and the roles played by parents and communities in keeping public systems operational". Psacharopoulos (2000, p.433) applauded the "meticulous accounting", and suggested that the approach should be emulated elsewhere. Ayres (2001, p.95) similarly stated that the book should "provide a valuable point of comparison for those intimately involved in educational policymaking in the region" (see also Mythili 2000; Clayton 2000; Coyne 2001; Patrinos 2002).

The present publication results from a study commissioned by the World Bank to assist in further development of primary and lower secondary schooling in Cambodia. The study on the one hand highlighted achievements of recent reforms, and on the other hand indicated continuing efforts that were needed. The scale and nature of household financing has major implications for socio-economic and rural/urban inequalities. This publication also exposes the significance of the parallel, shadow system of private tutoring which has major implications for the operation of the mainstream education system.

The main body of the book has nine parts. It begins by identifying themes and issues in a comparative framework. This is followed by presentation of the Cambodian social, economic and educational context. The next section turns to explanation of the methods through which data were collected for the present study. The book then documents household costs, comparing patterns in primary and lower secondary schooling and noting differences in urban, rural and remote areas. These findings are followed by a section on opportunity costs. The next section focuses on incomes received at the school level from the government and from other sources, which then permits comparison of the balance between household and government financing. The penultimate part presents policy implications, and the last part concludes.

Household Financing of Education: Comparative Perspectives

Changing International Views

The nature of household financing of education has attracted attention from a number of researchers in recent years (e.g. Bray 1996a; Penrose 1998; Boyle et al. 2002; Supriadi 2003; Tilak 2003). The comparative literature has highlighted wide ranges in the scale of household financing. In some settings all in-school costs are met by governments, and the out-of-school costs of uniforms, transport etc. are so small in proportion to both total schooling costs and total household incomes that they are not considered by analysts to deserve much attention. This is the case in many industrialised countries of Western Europe and North America, for example. Elsewhere, household expenses are so large that they comprise over half the total costs of schooling, even in public systems of education; and in poor societies the burden of costs on household budgets may be heavy. The earlier study on which the present book is based showed that Cambodia was one country in the latter category. Household costs at the primary level have since been reduced, though they remain high and are even more evident in secondary schools. Other Asian countries in which household costs are high include Myanmar (Mehrotra & Delamonica 1998), Vietnam (Truong et al. 1999), and parts of China (Bray et al. 2004); and comparable issues arise in Africa and other parts of the world (see e.g. Colclough et al. 2003).

Opinion on the desirability or otherwise of substantial household financing of education is mixed. Much depends on specific circumstances, but some generalities may be identified. Opponents of household financing point out that such financing exacerbates inequalities because rich households can afford payments more easily than poor ones. Since the quantity and quality of education received by a child is a very important determinant of that child's subsequent standard of living, many analysts have major misgivings about the fact that some households are able to give their children substantial head-starts which are denied to others. Increasing household costs at higher levels of education systems in turn raise drop-out rates, with the scale of the impact depending on the elasticity of the response to costs.

Commentators who view household financing more positively usually recognise this point, but argue that the problem cannot be avoided and that at least in some settings the merits of household financing outweigh the demerits. Such commentators may argue that education is a commodity like many others, and that households and communities have as much right to spend their money on education as they do on housing, clothes, food and other commodities. These commentators may be more tolerant of social inequalities, and may even argue that households which invest in education are doing a service to the whole society by increasing general levels of human capital.

A further factor concerns the capacity of governments to finance educational provision. In the societies where household financing is greatest, that feature is not usually the result of deliberate policy.

Rather, it is a default situation created by the governments' inability to meet all the needs which they would like to meet. Cambodia is in this category. The government certainly desires to do more for the people; but such action requires improved administrative capacity and greater income from taxation and other sources. Unless and until these are achieved, households find that if they want schooling of a reasonable quality – and in some cases, especially at post-primary levels, if they want schooling at all – then they must themselves provide much of the necessary resourcing.

Allied to this debate is an international shift in opinion on appropriate policies for educational financing. During the first four decades after the Second World War, the dominant feature of international pronouncements was that public education should be free of charge, especially at the level of basic education. Article 26 of the 1948 United Nations Declaration of Human Rights stated that:

> Everyone has the right to education. Education shall be free, at least in the elementary and fundamental stages.

Similarly, Principle 7 of the 1959 Declaration of the Rights of the Child stated that:

> The child is entitled to receive education, which shall be free and compulsory, at least in the early stages.

And Article 13 of the 1966 International Covenant on Economic, Social and Cultural Rights declared that:

> (a) Primary education shall be compulsory and available free to all.
> (b) Secondary education in its different forms … shall be made generally available and accessible to all by every appropriate means, and in particular by the progressive introduction of free education.
> (c) Higher education shall be made equally accessible to all, on the basis of capacity, by every appropriate means, and in particular by the progressive introduction of free education

However, general perceptions are now much more tolerant of the notion of cost-sharing, particularly in higher education. Indeed, at that level considerable evidence shows that fee-free education, far from promoting equity, is likely to exacerbate inequities because the proportion of students from rich families attending universities (and thus receiving public subsidies) is usually much greater than the proportion of students from poor families. The current dominant international view is that public institutions of higher education should charge at least some fees, but that the needs of the poor should be protected through grants and perhaps loans of various kinds (Tilak 1997; Woodhall 2003; Debande 2004).

At lower levels of education, fee-charging in public education is more difficult to justify. This is especially the case at the primary level, with secondary education arguably occupying an intermediate position on the spectrum. Most governments are keen to achieve universal education, and are therefore anxious to avoid any obstruction to enrolment and attendance. The goal of universal education is partly motivated by desire for economic development but is also strongly driven by concerns for social development and for equity. Advocates of fee-free education point out that government investment in fee-free primary education is likely to be much more pro-poor than government investment in higher levels of education (see e.g. Watkins 2000; Tomasevski 2003).

While these points have a strong justification, however, ideals must be tempered with reality, especially in poor countries. Although most governments would like to be able to provide fee-free primary education – and some, including Cambodia, even enshrine this in their constitutions – in many countries the practical realities of balancing the books require at least some contribution from households and communities.

Reflecting these realities was the fact that the Declaration of the World Conference on Education for All (WCEFA) did not include a statement that schooling should be free of charge. Instead, the Final Report of the Conference (WCEFA 1990a, p.31) included open discussion of fees; and Article 7 of the Declaration (WCEFA 1990b, p.7) stressed the importance of partnerships:

> National, regional and local educational authorities have a unique obligation to provide basic education for all, but they cannot be expected to supply every human, financial or organizational

requirement for this task. New and revitalized partnerships at all levels will be necessary … [including] partnerships between government and non-governmental organizations, the private sector, local communities, religious groups, and families.

This type of statement, moreover, has relevance to prosperous societies as well as poor ones. The Government of Singapore is certainly rich enough to be able to provide all the resources needed to educate the country's children. However, even the Singaporean Government encourages some household and community financing. This is not so much for financial reasons as because the partnership raises the level of family and community commitment to the educational processes. In 1998, the government launched a scheme called COMPASS, which was an acronym for COMmunity and PArents in Support of Schools (Manzon 2004). It built on older initiatives (see e.g. Tan 1995, p.34) which pointed out that the government cannot do everything by itself, and that communities can greatly contribute to the effectiveness of educational processes. Similar findings have been presented with respect to Philippines by Jimenez and Paqueo (1996), and with respect to Indonesia by James et al. (1996). The same sorts of factors may be evident in Cambodia. Households which make at least some contribution to schools may take a greater interest in those schools than would be the case if everything was provided free of charge.

Nevertheless, in contrast to the 1990 World Conference on Education for All, the follow-up World Education Forum (WEF) convened a decade later in Dakar, Senegal, returned to the refrain that primary education should be free and compulsory, and added that the education should be of good quality (WEF 2000, p.15):

All children must have the opportunity to fulfil their right to quality education in schools or alternative programmes at whatever level is considered 'basic'. All states must fulfil their obligation to offer free and compulsory primary education…. For the millions of children living in poverty, who suffer multiple disadvantages, there must be an unequivocal commitment that education be free of tuition and other fees, and that everything possible be done to reduce or eliminate costs such as those for learning materials, uniforms, school meals and transport. Wider social policies, interventions and incentives should be used to mitigate indirect opportunity costs of attending school. No one should be denied the opportunity to complete a good quality primary education because it is unaffordable.

Yet while such visionary statements can have value, there is a danger in rhetoric which implies that 'one size fits all'. Further, education is never free in the sense that it does not have to be paid for by somebody, and in poor countries the resource crunch is an inescapable reality. In most societies, the main source of revenue for public education is taxation; but Cambodia and other countries do not have strong mechanisms for securing taxation revenues. This type of issue was not squarely addressed by the World Education Forum, which remained largely at the level of exhortation. Further, while it seems eminently desirable to have fee-free education for poor households, it is less obvious that education should be free of charge for the middle-income and rich. Matters are therefore more complex than might be discerned from the statements of the World Education Forum and some other bodies.

Mechanisms and Types of Household Financing

In most systems, the most obvious and direct form of revenue generation by schools is through fees. Often, these are general fees, but sometimes they are specified for books, repairs, extra-curricular activities, etc. (see e.g. King 1997, p.175; Marchand 2000, pp.127-140; Lerotholi 2001, pp.52-66). Sometimes school authorities waive fees for poor children, or grant reductions to families with more than one child in school. As Urwick (2002, p.141) noted with reference to Nigeria, fees commonly have a negotiated status.

When schools are prohibited from charging fees, they may use euphemisms such as 'levies' or 'contributions', and demand cash payments in other ways. The Cambodian data on primary schools presented in the 1999 book (Bray 1999a) included many examples, which had parallels elsewhere, of per-pupil payments for construction, repairs and equipment. Other payments were made for stationery, examination papers, electricity and many other items. These household payments had been considerably reduced by 2004, chiefly through government initiatives.

Turning to out-of-school costs, many schools throughout the world require households to purchase uniforms and some families also pay for school meals. Children need clothes and food whether they go to school or not. However, some uniforms cost more than other clothes, particularly when they include shoes and have other specialist demands, e.g. for sports. School meals may also be more costly than home-cooked ones, though that is not always the case. One study in Myanmar found that uniforms, school bags and clothing consumed 53.7 per cent of total household expenditures on primary schooling, while books and stationery consumed 7.5 per cent, and pocket money consumed 30.0 per cent (Evans & Rorris 1994, pp.46, 55, 63). The pocket money was mainly used for snacks and other small items. The researchers did not originally consider pocket money to be a cost of schooling, but parents clearly saw it as an educational expense and independently added it as a specific category. Similar findings have been recorded in Ghana, where food was reported in 1995 to form 69.5 per cent of household expenditures on primary education (Penrose 1998, p.60). Transport is also commonly a major household expense, especially at the post-primary level. Pocket money and transport are sometimes omitted from estimates of the cost of education, but are included in the present study on the grounds that they are certainly seen by households, even if not always by ministries of education, as part of the cost. The costs of both pocket money and transport are generally higher at secondary than primary education, first because older children eat more snacks and have greater demands for pocket money, and second because secondary schools are commonly more distant than primary schools from pupils' homes.

A further item which is a major expense in Cambodia and also in some other countries (see e.g. Bray 1999b, 2003a; Foondun 2002; Yoo 2002; Kwok 2004) is supplementary tutoring. In many settings this would be called an out-of-school expense because the tutoring would be in specially designated premises or in the tutors' or students' homes. In Cambodia, much of the tutoring is in the students' own schools and is given by their own teachers. Thus when the official school day ends, the unofficial school day begins – with the same teachers and the same pupils occupying the same desks in the same classrooms. Supplementary tutoring is a particularly significant item of household expenditure in towns, but may also be found in rural areas.

The concept of household financing overlaps with that of community financing. Communities have a broader locus of decision-making, and in some settings are major forces in the education sector (see e.g. Bray with Lillis 1988; Annigeri 1998; Francis et al. 1998; Miller-Grandvaux & Yoder 2002). In Cambodia, the role of village bodies and Buddhist pagodas has long been significant (Shimizu 1999), though at the beginning of the 21st century in the education sector this role appeared to have reduced compared with that in earlier decades.

Cambodia: Society, Economy and Education

Historical Perspectives

Cambodia has had a turbulent past, which has included many dramatic transitions. Several of these transitions have implications for education, including its financing. A few observations about the past assist with understanding of the present.

Cambodia gained Independence from the French in 1953. During the colonial era, the government-sponsored education system was small and primarily oriented to the needs of an élite. However, Cambodia's long tradition of education for boys in its Buddhist pagodas, financed primarily from contributions by villagers, continued in parallel with the colonial schools. From 1911 onwards, some of these pagoda schools were secularised. They were popular among Cambodians, especially in rural areas, and were used by the colonial regime to extend the availability of education (Clayton 1995, p.8; Dy 2004, p.92). In the 1930s, a further model was introduced in which monks were trained in the methods of Franco-Cambodian education and then sent back to their schools which were designated 'modernised' pagoda schools. The modernised pagoda schools offered a curriculum similar to that of Franco-Cambodian elementary schools except that all courses were in Khmer. Ayres (2003, pp.24-25) remarked that:

> It could easily be argued that the "modernized" temple [pagoda] schools were a fine example of "association," in which colonial ideas and native institutions were blended in harmony. A more cynical and possibly realistic assessment is that the modernization of

the temple schools was a financially prudent move for the French. Rather than finance an entire education system, they were able to rely on existing teaching staff and existing infrastructure, financed by the villages themselves.

In this sense, balance of financing between the state and households has a long history.

The post-Independence era, as elsewhere (see e.g. Thompson 1981; Tilak 1994a), brought pressure to expand the education system, chiefly through the state machinery though with support from village communities particularly in construction of buildings. Modernised pagoda schools continued to operate in parallel to state schools, but the latter were given greater emphasis. Government budgets were severely stretched, though they were supplemented by external aid. Private schools flourished, particularly during the 1960s. Education was allocated a much greater percentage of the government budget than was the case in the 1990s, in some years gaining over 20.0 per cent (Chandler 1994, p.199); and teachers were well paid, especially in comparison with other professions (Tilak 1994b, p.59). In 1970, public expenditure on education formed 5.8 per cent of Gross National Product (Asian Development Bank [ADB] 1996, p.73).

The early and mid-1970s brought abrupt change, most dramatically with the ascendance of the Khmer Rouge and the establishment in 1975 of what later became known as the Pol Pot regime. During the period 1975-79, almost all schools were closed and in many cases their contents were destroyed. Teachers were singled out for persecution in an attempt to obliterate pre-revolutionary modes of thinking. As noted by the United Nations Development Programme [UNDP] (1997, p.2), Cambodia is:

> probably the only country in the world that experienced (during the Khmer Rouge years of 1975-79) not merely genocide on a scale hitherto unseen, but deliberate state-sponsored destruction of economic, social and human capital. Anywhere from one to two million people lost their lives due to torture, execution, disease, and starvation.

The reconstruction during the 1980s under Vietnamese advice and support followed socialist models. The ADB (1996, p.1) described the results of these and subsequent efforts as the rise of "a phoenix from the ashes". Households and communities played a major role in school construction during the 1980s, but the socialist system had no place for either monastery schools or private institutions.

Following the official abandonment of socialism in 1991, private schools were once again permitted. No pagoda schools of the type that had been common prior to 1970 were re-established during the 1990s, though 19.1 per cent of (secular) primary schools in 2001/02 were located within the compounds of pagodas (MoEYS 2002c, p.1). Despite the operation of the market economy, in 2001/02 private schools served less than 1.0 per cent of primary school enrolment. Among the 86 private primary schools existing in that year, many catered for minorities and foreign groups and only eight used Khmer as the medium of instruction (MoEYS 2003, p.17).

In summary, household and community financing of education has long roots in Cambodia, but different eras have brought different emphases. Household and community resources were major inputs during both the colonial and the initial post-colonial eras, though little empirical data exists on the nature or dynamics of those inputs. During the 1960s, government budgets supported education much more fully than was the case in the 1990s. The Pol Pot regime of 1975-79 brought household and community financing of education practically to a stop; but activities were revived during the 1980s, and took new directions from the early 1990s. They took further new directions at the beginning of the present century.

Contemporary Social and Economic Features

Cambodia is divided into 20 provinces plus four municipalities (Kep, Pailin, Phnom Penh and Sihanoukville). Provinces are subdivided into districts, which total 185, and the country has approximately 13,400 villages. As one would expect, levels of development vary widely in different parts of the country.

Within the total population of approximately 13 million people, about 95 per cent are Khmers, most of whom are Buddhists. Minority groups include Cham-Malays, Vietnamese, Chinese, Thais, Laotians, and members of hill tribes. The plains are the most densely populated areas, while the plateaux and mountain regions are the least densely populated.

At the national level, Cambodia's political framework has had some stability since the ascendance of the Cambodian People's Party in the second half of the 1990s (Zasloff 2002; Sodhy 2004). However, major tensions remained; and the government could only operate through a coalition of factions which did not have a history of collaborating well with each other. The system had sufficient stability to assure external donors that their resources would be put to appropriate use, but policy-making and policy-implementation were not always straightforward in the situation of balances between competing factions.

Political factors have also of course had an influence on economics. The Cambodian currency, the riel, had been unstable during much of the 1990s and before, but stabilised at the end of 1990s and remained stable during the initial years of the new decade. Thus from 1998 to the time of the research in 2004, the exchange rate was stable at approximately US$1 = 4,000 riels. At the same time, the dollar itself circulated widely, particularly in urban areas. This was chiefly a legacy from the period in which the riel was unstable.

Political and economic matters have also had an impact on broader dimensions of development. The UNDP ranks countries on a Human Development Index which is based on life expectancies, literacy rates, enrolment rates in primary, secondary and tertiary education, and per capita incomes. In 1995, Cambodia was grouped with the low-human-development countries: number 153 out of 174 countries (UNDP 1995, p.157). However, in 2004 Cambodia was grouped with the medium-human-development countries, albeit towards the low end of that group: number 130 out of 177 countries (UNDP 2004, p.141). Improvements had been achieved in all indicators which contributed to the Human Development Index, and particularly the domain of education.

Despite these improvements, a considerable proportion of the population, especially in rural areas, lives in poverty. Poverty may have many dimensions (Cambodia 2002, p.94), but the present study is mainly concerned with economic factors and income levels. Figure 1 is a poverty map prepared by the World Food Programme (WFP) using a number of sources of data. It is important to note that communes that are larger in area are also more sparsely populated and tend to have

Balancing the Books

higher proportions of poor households. The poverty status of large communes therefore dominates a map based on the proportion of poor households (see also Ondrusek 2002, pp.15-17; World Food Programme 2002).

Figure 1: Poverty Rates by Commune, Cambodia

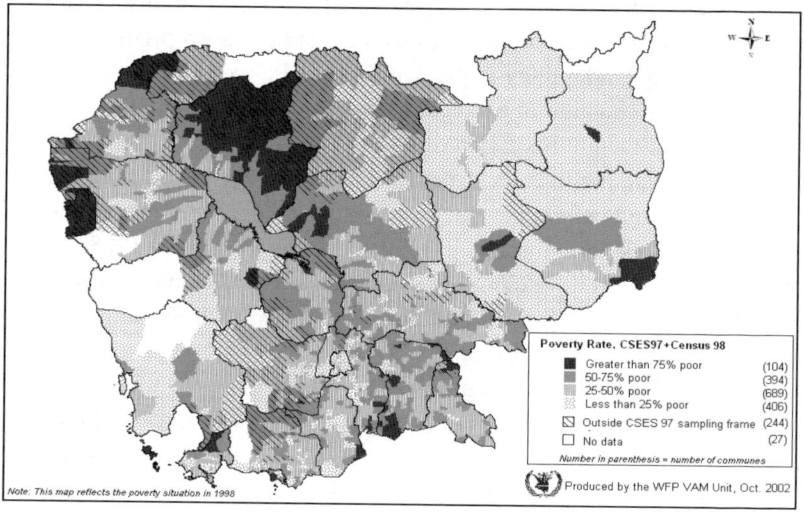

The government in collaboration with international partners has also calculated poverty lines below which individuals are assumed to have inadequate incomes to consume food providing at least 2,100 calories per day and essential non-food items such as shelter and clothing. The poverty lines in rural areas are lower than in urban areas, reflecting different costs of living. Table 1 shows the monetary value of poverty lines calculated from the 1999 poverty survey. It shows separately the food poverty lines, which do not take account of non-food consumption, and the overall poverty lines; and it suggests that over half the rural population was living below the overall poverty line. These patterns have major implications for the ability of households to contribute to the costs of schooling.

Table 1: Poverty Lines by Region, Cambodia, 1999 (Income per Day)

	Food Poverty Line (FPL)		Overall Poverty Line (OPL)		% of population estimated to be below the poverty lines*	
	Riels	US$	Riels	US$	FPL	OPL
Phnom Penh	1,737	0.45	2,470	0.63	5.2	14.6
Other Urban	1,583	0.41	2,093	0.54	28.4	42.4
Rural	1,379	0.35	1,777	0.46	31.5	56.1

* Based on both rounds of the 1999 Cambodia Socio-Economic Survey

Source: Council for Social Development (2002), pp.31, 32.

Since the early 1990s, Cambodia has received considerable resources for all sectors from international aid. Between 1994 and 1997, aid to education expanded from US$29.1 million to US$53.2 million (Chuor & Sereyrath 2004, p.39). It dipped as a result of Cambodia's 1997 political crisis (Zasloff 2002), but in every year from 1994 to 1999 foreign aid to education exceeded the government budget for education, sometimes by a considerable margin. Subsequently the government budget grew, but donor activities remained very important both within and beyond the government budget (MoEYS 2003, p.96). Education sector inputs by donors and external lending agencies amounted to US$44.6 million in 2002 (Chuor & Sereyrath 2004, p.40), of which the largest components came from the ADB (31.9%), the World Bank (16.8%), UNICEF (14.0%), and the Japan International Cooperation Agency (12.4%).

The external resources have been especially important to Cambodia because of the government's limited capacity to generate domestic revenues. The World Bank pointed out in 1995 (p.17) that Cambodia's ratio of taxation to Gross Domestic Product (GDP), at 6.0 per cent in 1994, was very low compared with that of neighbouring countries. In Vietnam, for example, the ratio was 17.4 per cent (1993), and in Lao People's Democratic Republic it was 9.1 per cent. Elsewhere in the region the ratio was even higher, for example reaching 18.0 per cent in Sri Lanka and 20.6 per cent in Malaysia in 1995 (World Bank 1997, pp.240-241). Considerable progress was made in the second half of the 1990s, but a joint report by the World Bank and the Asian Development

Bank (2003, p.5) still pointed out that "Cambodia's fiscal revenue ratios, especially tax revenue, remain among the lowest in the world". Table 2 compares Cambodia's taxation revenue structure in 2001 with that in a number of other low-income countries which are classified by the International Monetary Fund as being appropriate for low-interest loans under the Poverty Reduction & Growth Facility (PRGF). The column on taxation revenue as a percentage of GDP shows that Cambodia was considerably below the Asian and African averages, and in this table only Bangladesh and Niger had lower percentages. The figure on total government revenue as a percentage of GDP, which includes non-taxation and capital revenue, was also considerably below average. This had implications for government financing of education as much as for other sectors.

Table 2: Taxation Revenues in Cambodia and Selected Other Countries

	Per capita GDP (US$)	Total government revenue as % of GDP	Taxation revenue as % of GDP
Cambodia	259	11.7	8.4
PRGF Asian countries	427	16.2	12.8
Bangladesh	370	8.6	7.1
Lao People's Democratic Republic	310	11.4	9.2
Nepal	240	11.2	9.2
Sri Lanka	830	17.0	14.7
Vietnam	410	20.6	15.6
Mongolia	400	28.5	20.8
PRGF African Countries	323	17.6	13.7
Cameroon	570	17.8	12.2
Guinea Bissau	160	19.5	10.8
Mali	210	14.7	14.0
Niger	170	8.9	8.3
Tanzania	280	11.8	10.6
Togo	270	13.8	12.3

Cambodian data are for 2001. Data for other countries are an average of 1999-2001.

Source: World Bank & Asian Development Bank (2003), p.6.

The Education System

The main part of Cambodia's education system has a 6+3+3 structure: six years of primary schooling are followed by three years of lower secondary schooling and three years of upper secondary schooling. In addition, some children attend pre-schools; and some students proceed to university and other post-secondary studies.

Table 3 presents data on school enrolments from 1996/97 to 2003/04, and shows remarkable growth. During the period, primary school enrolments expanded by 36.5 per cent, and lower secondary school enrolments doubled. At the primary level, especially impressive jumps in enrolments were achieved in 1999/00, 2000/01 and 2001/02, when the average annual growth was 10.2 per cent. At the lower secondary level, achievements were even more dramatic, with an average annual expansion between 1999/00 and 2003/04 of 24.2 per cent. Policy interventions concerning household financing of education, in conjunction with a very strong enrolment campaign by the government, were major instruments to achieve such gains. With such advances, Cambodia was rapidly closing the gap caused by earlier neglect of education.

Table 3: School Enrolments, Cambodia, 1996/97 – 2003/04

	1996/97	1997/98	1998/99	1999/00
Primary	1,918,985	2,011,772	2,094,000	2,211,738
Lower secondary	265,895	229,102	226,057	233,278
Upper secondary	61,671	73,849	82,110	108,213

	2000/01	2001/02	2002/03	2003/04
Primary	2,408,109	2,705,453	2,747,411	2,747,080
Lower secondary	283,578	351,635	415,703	459,986
Upper secondary	105,086	113,404	128,182	153,758

Source: MoEYS, Education Management Information System, various years.

To supplement these figures, Table 4 shows statistics on schools, enrolments and teachers in 2003/04. Male pupils outnumbered females at all levels and by increasing proportions at higher levels of the system.

Since more girls were out of school than boys, the cost and other barriers to enrolment of girls demanded particular attention.

Table 4: Numbers of Schools, Pupils and Teachers, 2003/04

	Schools	—— Pupils ——		—— Teachers ——	
		Total	% female	Total	% female
Primary	6,063	2,747,080	47.0	49,603	40.7
Lower secondary	688	459,986	41.9	18,589	33.2
Upper secondary	212	153,758	35.8	5,630	25.3

Source: MoEYS (2004a), p.1.

A major issue since the 1990s has concerned the low level of teachers' salaries. In 1993, teachers were earning, on average, just US$6 per month from their official salaries. To raise these earnings, in 1994 the government gave a general 20 per cent salary rise for civil servants plus a 'prime pédagogique' of US$8 per month to teachers and other education officers (ADB 1996, p.81). This increased average teachers' earnings, including allowances, to the equivalent of US$23 per month. While this was a considerable improvement, the figure remained very low. A further 20 per cent salary increase approved in 1998 helped ameliorate the situation; but even after this increase, salaries remained very low. Primary teachers received less than secondary ones; and junior teachers received less than senior ones. Even at the top end of the scale, the salary was far from adequate to meet family needs.

The matter was raised in the 2002 Education Sector Support Program (ESSP) Review, which stated (MoEYS 2002a, p.5) that:

> The salary issue continues to be a major weakness in the broad financial planning and implementation of the reforms. This is especially so for school staff and for primary staff in particular. It has wider ramifications because informal fees collected by teachers continue to be a barrier for poor families. However, part of parental contributions to school costs are in fact payments to teachers. Salary increases provide justification for reducing or abolishing such fees. The current projections for the education

wage bill are not realistic because they will not accommodate the pay rise policy....

There is no adequate legal foundation for the pay reform in the whole civil service. Therefore, there is no certainty for the teachers and other personnel working in the education sector about their future.... There is no effective inter-ministerial mechanism to agree crucial decisions, including examining the full impact on medium term macro and sectoral salary envelopes.

A year later, the 2003 ESSP Review (MoEYS 2003, p.31) noted the existence of a wider Strategic Civil Service Reform plan, and stated that the MoEYS had "begun to explore" financing options which would enable it to raise education personnel incomes above those of other civil servants. However, the document subsequently stressed the need to maintain a high non-wage spending share (at that time 45-55%), in part through containment of education salaries growth in line with broader civil service pay reform. The subsequent *Education Strategic Plan 2004/08* (MoEYS 2004b, p.31) altered these targets for non-wage spending, envisaging a decrease from 40 per cent in 2004 to 32 per cent in 2008. This was partly because the document again stressed the need to increase teachers' salaries, with primary teachers as first priority (MoEYS 2004b pp.16, 19, 23). However, the document was arguably over-optimistic in its assessment of the prospects for extra government revenue. Projections (p.49) were based on an assumption of annual economic growth of 6.5 per cent in the five years from 2004 to 2008, and the document did not specifically address issues of taxation rates.

Meanwhile, in 2003/04 primary school teachers at the mid-point of the official salary scale earned just 149,200 riels (US$37.30) per month, with a range on the scale from 130,800 to 168,000 riels. Their counterparts in lower secondary schools received 152,500 riels (US$38.10) per month, with a range from 133,800 to 171,600 riels. Moreover, salaries were often delivered late (Naren & Collins 2004). Table 1 recorded an overall poverty line at 1999 prices for urban areas of 2,470 riels (US$0.63) per day, i.e. on a 30-day month 74,100 riels (US$18.90) per month. On this ratio, a primary school teacher in Phnom Penh on the mid-point of the scale who had to support just one person in addition to her/himself on the official salary would be living on the 1999 poverty line. Lower secondary school teachers would not be much better off. Teachers outside Phnom Penh had lower costs of living, but were still far from comfortable. Supplements could be gained by teaching multi-grade and double-shift classes, accepting postings in difficult areas, examining in the national examinations, and undertaking remedial classes in the summer months; but these supplements still left teaching as a severely underpaid profession.

Budgetary Allocations for Education

During the 1990s, the proportion of the government budget allocated to education was very low by international standards. For example, during the period 1994-97, education was budgeted to receive between 8.4 and 9.6 per cent of total government spending, and in real terms funding for education from government sources fell between 1995 and 1997 (Pheng et al. 2001, p.26). In most countries of the region, education was allo-cated well over 10 per cent, and in a few countries the figure exceeded 20 per cent (Bray 2004, p.7). Further, in Cambodia actual expenditures on social services were often lower than the budgeted amounts. By con-trast, defence and security received 204 per cent of their budgeted allo-cation in 1994, and 106 per cent in 1997 (Pheng et al. 2001, p.27).

This pattern was radically altered in the initial years of the new decade. As a proportion of GDP, treasury-executed expenditure on edu-cation, which had been 1.0 per cent in 1996, and 0.9 per cent in 1997 and 1998, reached 2.0 per cent in 2003 (World Bank & Asian Devel-opment Bank 2003, p.13). Conversely, during the same period the pro-portion allocated to defence fell from 3.5 per cent to 1.7 per cent. In US dollar terms, treasury-executed expenditures on education increased from US$31.0 million in 1996 to US$75.8 million in 2003 (World Bank & Asian Development Bank 2003, p.15). As a percentage of the total government recurrent budget, the share for education rose from 13.9 per cent in 2000 to 18.2 per cent in 2002 and then 19.1 per cent in 2004; and the proposed target for 2006 was as high as 22.2 per cent (MoEYS 2003, p.91).

Table 5 shows that a large proportion of the increase in government funds was in the non-wage recurrent sector. As a result of this growth, wages as a proportion of total recurrent expenditure decreased from 73.0 per cent in 2000 to 57.9 per cent in 2003. Capital expenditures also declined in absolute as well as proportional terms, chiefly because of the reduction in externally-financed capital expenditures routed through the government budget.

Table 5: Public Expenditures on Education, 2000-03 (Million Riels)

	2000	2001	2002	2003
Recurrent Expenditures	165,815	212,205	286,200	332,999
Wages	121,028	132,088	160,792	192,707
Non-Wages	44,787	80,117	125,408	140,292
- Administration	37,736	47,920	55,090	53,320
- Priority Action Programme	2,716	28,088	64,303	80,800
- Subsidies	4,335	4,109	6,015	6,172
Wages as % of total recurrent	73.0%	62.2%	56.2%	57.9%
Capital Expenditures	162,384	131,984	94,700	89,700
Government	4,045	17,343	4,000	4,000
Externally financed	158,339	114,634	90,700	85,700
Total Public Expenditures	328,119	344,189	380,900	422,699

Source: Ministry of Economy & Finance, Phnom Penh.

Within the non-wage sector, the most dramatic increase was in the Priority Action Programme (PAP), which was launched on a pilot basis in 10 provinces in 2000. A specific purpose of this pilot was "to reduce the cost burden on the poorest families to increase participation of their children in grades 1-9" (MoEYS 2001a, p.1). The scheme was expanded to cover the whole country in 2001, and elaborated to include focus on other parts of the education system. The PAPs channelled money directly from the Ministry of Economy & Finance to different sections of the Ministry of Education, Youth & Sport. In 2004, 12 PAPs existed, of which the most relevant to this study were:

- *PAP 1: Education Service Efficiency.* This programme focused on providing equitable access and improved quality and efficiency of the education service through improved utilisation of MOEYS personnel. Allowances were given through

PAP 1 to teachers in difficult areas, particularly ones with ethnic minorities, and to teachers responsible for multi-grade and double-shift classes.

- *PAP 2: Primary Education Quality and Efficiency.* This programme aimed to increase enrolment through school operational budgets. In 2001, the government announced that registration and other charges on households were prohibited, and that the income that would have been provided by these charges would instead be provided by the PAP 2. A second component of the programme aimed to increase grade progression and reduce repetition and drop-out through remedial classes. Guidelines for use of operational budgets were designed to ensure availability of school supplies, encourage minor repairs, and improve the overall school environment.

- *PAP 3: Secondary Education Quality and Efficiency.* This programme included provision of school operating budgets to over 550 lower secondary schools. The operational budgets were linked to MoEYS policy for abolishing start-of-year fees, as a strategy to reduce the burden on parents and to enhance equitable access.

- *PAP 12: Scholarships and Incentives for Equitable Access.* A major component of this programme was a scholarship scheme for lower secondary students, targeted particularly at girls in poor areas.

The PAPs have had a major impact, though their effectiveness was impaired by problems of cash flow. This problem was highlighted in the evaluation of the initial pilot in 2000 (MoEYS 2001a, p.3), and had still not been solved two years later. Table 6 shows that overall, only 46.6 per cent of PAP funds allocated in 2002 were released. The figure for PAP 2 was 61.7 per cent, but for PAP 3 it was 59.8 per cent and for PAP 1 it was only 32.0 per cent. The MoEYS was very conscious of this performance, and had taken steps to increase disbursement flows. At the same time, the MoEYS recognised that some difficulties arose from management capacity which could not be instantly resolved, and that "stakeholders have to be realistic in their expectations alongside progressive capacity building" (MoEYS 2003, p.29).

Table 6: PAP Allocations and Releases, 2002 (Million Riels)

	Allocated	*Released*	*% Released*
PAP 1: Education Service Efficiency	10,530	3,371	32.0
PAP 2: Primary Education Quality and Efficiency	23,918	14,760	61.7
PAP 3: Secondary Education Quality and Efficiency	7,386	4,415	59.8
PAP 4: Technical & Vocational Education Quality Efficiency	1,576	940	59.6
PAP 5: Quality and Efficiency of Higher Education	101	51	50.5
PAP 6: Continuous Teacher Development	6,557	3,938	60.1
PAP 7: Sustainable Provision of Core Instructional Materials	13,348	3,207	24.0
PAP 8: Expansion of Nonformal Education	1,998	808	40.4
PAP 9: Youth HIV/AIDS Awareness	601	179	29.8
PAP 10: Sports Development			
PAP 11: Strengthened Monitoring Systems	401	189	47.1
PAP 12: Scholarships and Incentives for Equitable Access	6,730	2,260	33.6
Total	*73,147*	*34,118*	*46.6*

Source: MoEYS (2003), p.33.

School Enrolment Rates

The government has made significant strides in its push towards Education for All (EFA), and the PAPs have been among the instruments to achieve this. Most obvious has been the use of the PAPs to provide government resources to schools in order to reduce the financial burden on households. This instrument is of major relevance to the present study, and was accompanied in 2001 by a Ministerial statement that teachers who continued to accept informal payments would be the object of sanctions (MoEYS 2001b).

In addition, the pilot PAP in 2000 included measures to reduce repetition, especially in the initial grades, in order to release space for new enrolments. Part of the strategy for reducing repetition was the operation of a special remedial class in the summer months, for which teachers received financial remuneration. As a result of these strategies, the promotion rate for Grade 1 increased from around 54 per cent in 1999 to 82 per cent in 2000, while the promotion rate for Grade 2 increased from 67 to 83 per cent.

These various measures resulted in dramatic expansion of overall primary enrolments, as shown in Table 3. As primary-level enrolments expanded, pressure increased at the lower secondary level. Some of this demand was met, and lower secondary enrolments also expanded dramatically. The MoEYS (2004b, p.8) estimated the net primary school enrolment rate in 2002/03 at 88.9 per cent for both sexes, though MoEYS estimates of enrolment rates have been rather higher than those of household surveys (World Bank 2004, p.13). Further, at lower secondary level even the MoEYS estimated the net enrolment rate at only 19.1 per cent. As Bredenberg (2003, p.1) pointed out, following realisation of considerable progress in primary schooling, lower secondary education was the next great frontier.

At the primary level (and then in due course at the lower secondary level), achievement of the enrolment targets was assisted for a short period by demographic factors. Figure 2 shows Cambodia's unique population structure, which reflects the tragic loss of life during the Khmer Rouge period of the 1970s and the ensuing civil war. In 2003, the population in the 25-29 age group was much smaller than either the immediately older or the younger cohorts. Since this group was in the prime period for child-bearing, the population in the age-group 0-4 was also smaller than its predecessors. Similarly, the population aged 5-9 was rather smaller than the population aged 10-14. As these small cohorts entered the primary and then secondary school age groups, pressure on school places was relieved and enrolment rates could reach higher levels. However, this was only expected to be a short-term phenomenon. The trough in numbers of children aged 6-11 was calculated to be in 2004, after which numbers would again rise. By 2008 numbers in this age group were expected to exceed the 1998 level, and to continue to rise thereafter.

Also important to note are the large proportions of children who are older than the standard, either because of late entry or because of slow progression through the system because of repetition and/or drop-out and re-entry. The 2001 Cambodia Child Labour Survey (CCLS) suggested that 72.2 per cent of children who entered school for the first time were older than six, and the average age for lower secondary school students was 15.8 (World Bank 2004, p.13). Among the Grade 1 entrants, a notable proportion of the over-age pupils were from poor households. According to CCLS data, in 2001 76.2 per cent of Grade 1 pupils in the poorest quintile were over-age, compared with 53.4 per cent in the richest quintile. Also, over-age enrolments were more common in rural than urban areas, respective figures being 74.4 and 62.2 per cent (World Bank 2004, p.73).

Figure 2: Population Pyramid, Cambodia, 2003

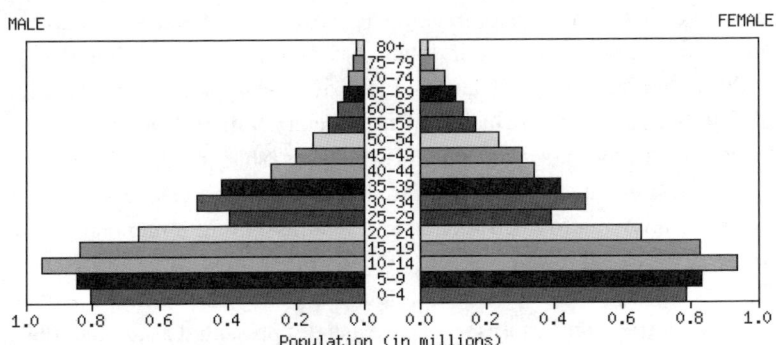

Source: Projection from 1998 census.

Methods of Data Collection

Definitions and Approaches

In all settings, data on household expenditures on education and other items are difficult to collect (Howes & Lanjouw 1997; Glewwe 2000). This is for several reasons. First, households may choose to under-report or over-report expenditures depending on what purpose is perceived for the data collection. If households expect to be reimbursed for expenditures by the government or other agencies, they are likely to present high figures; but if households do not wish to be seen as spending large amounts, e.g. because that could be viewed as purchasing advantages for their children or exposing themselves to higher taxation, they tend to present low figures.

Second, conceptions of what should be included in calculations may vary. For example, as indicated above, pocket money for purchase of snacks during the school day might be seen as a cost of education or might not. Similar remarks apply to clothing and means of transport such as bicycles. Surveys need to set clear definitions and then to communicate those definitions to all relevant people.

Third, survey data are normally collected through interviews and questionnaires. However, interviewees and questionnaire-respondents do not always have clear pictures of costs. In some households difficulties arise from the separate roles of individual members – e.g. fathers may take different decision-making roles from mothers. Alternatively, uncles, aunts, elder siblings or others may be involved in different ways, with no single individuals having clear overviews. Further, calculation of full costs requires inclusion of a monetary value of goods and services which have not been purchased with cash, including labour and agricultural or other produce donated to schools and teachers. Identification of amounts of such inputs, and then assigning a monetary value to them, may not be easy.

A further difficulty is that although according to normal academic and accounting conventions, costs are usually presented as annual totals, households may not themselves calculate costs on an annual basis. Seasonal variations may be considerable, and interviewees may not make accurate calculations of yearly totals which allow for such variations. The period of the year in which data are collected may significantly influence the nature of the data.

Finally, calculation of full costs requires assessment of opportunity costs, particularly the incomes foregone because children are in school. Such assessment is difficult because it relies on assumptions first about what the children would have been doing had they not been in school, and second about the economic value of those activities. Different prices need to be set for children of different ages and genders, and for households in urban, rural and remote locations with different forms of economic production.

To tackle such problems, in ideal circumstances household costs are best estimated through careful sampling which takes into account a full range of socio-economic and regional differences. Surveys may then be conducted by trained enumerators who are clear in their definitions, speak local languages, ask appropriate questions, record answers accurately, and are persistent in their efforts. Ideally, the data from such enumerators would then be cross-checked, coded and analysed, to provide reliable estimates not only for the country as a whole but also for sub-categories.

The main difficulty with such an approach is that it is costly in both money and personnel. Rigorous household surveys demand considerable finance and availability of appropriate enumerators, trainers, coders and tabulators. In addition, strict random sampling requires the ability to travel anywhere in the country to collect the necessary data.

Sampling and Data Collection

In 1997/98, when the original study of household costs was conducted (Bray 1999a), Cambodia's political and social circumstances precluded travel to all parts of the country, and inadequate financial and human resources were available for a rigorous household survey. Data for the original study were therefore collected through a method which was considered less than ideal but adequate for the purpose. The research for Phase 1 at that time focused on two sites, one rural and the other urban. Data were collected through questionnaires and follow-up discussion with personnel from nine schools in each location. School directors (headteachers) were asked to complete the questionnaires and then to bring their data to workshops which lasted a full day in each case. In addition separate workshops, also with questionnaires, were organised for parents to report and discuss the costs of schooling. The data from the parents amplified and helped confirm or modify the data received from the schools. Detailed notes of the workshop discussions were kept, to supplement the data in the questionnaires.

For Phase 2 in the 1997/98 study, six further workshops, each catering for between eight and 10 schools, were held in different provinces. The sites were selected to provide a range of urban and rural locations with prosperous and impoverished communities. Respondents were again asked to complete questionnaires in advance, and to bring their completed questionnaires to the workshops for discussion and checking. The questionnaire used for Phase 2 was a modified version of that used for Phase 1. To gain additional qualitative data, eight detailed case studies were conducted in a further four provinces. Two schools in each province were

selected with a range of features. Some were urban while others were
rural, and the schools had varying reputations for strength in household
and community financing. The research teams were particularly interested
in the dynamics of operation.

In 2004, the starting point was the set of primary schools and their
communities surveyed in 1997/98. These were then supplemented by a
group of lower secondary schools. The original instruments were modified in the light of experience six years previously, and in each province
two focus sites were selected – one urban (or semi-urban) and the other
rural. The resulting sample covered the 11 provinces and one municipal-
ity of the 1997/98 sample, namely Banteay Meanchey, Battambang,
Kampot, Kampong Cham, Kampong Speu, Kampong Thom, Kandal,
Phnom Penh, Ratanakiri, Stung Treng, Svay Rieng, and Takeo. The
focus group discussions were in seven of the provinces plus Phnom
Penh. The survey covered 77 primary and 39 lower secondary schools
(Table 7).

Table 7: Sample of Schools and Focus Sites, 2004

Province/ Municipality	No. of primary schools surveyed	No. of lower secondary schools surveyed	Number of focus sites	Number of focus group discussions
Banteay Meanchey	8	4	2	8
Battambang	8	4	2	8
Kampot	8	4	2	8
Kandal	9	4	2	8
Phnom Penh	9	4	2	8
Ratanakiri	8	3	2	8
Svay Rieng	10	4	2	8
Takeo	9	4	2	8
Kampong Cham	2	2	-	-
Kampong Speu	2	2	-	-
Kampong Thom	2	2	-	-
Stung Treng	2	2	-	-
Total	*77*	*39*	*16*	*64*

The sampling design for the focus group discussions, which identified both urban (including semi-urban) and rural (including remote) sites, recognised that the terms urban and rural may have rather variable meanings. Thus Ratanakiri for example is a remote province, and Banlung, its headquarters, may be described as urban in comparison with the rest of the province but is much smaller than its counterparts in most other provinces. The sample did not include as strong a representation of remote regions as might have been desired, but nevertheless covered a range of conditions around the country. Each site for focus group discussions included a primary school that fed into a lower secondary school.

Another difference between 1997/98 and 2004 was in the nature of the teams collecting data. In 1997/98, data were collected by personnel from UNICEF, UNESCO and the MoEYS. UNESCO and UNICEF were involved because they had provided the initial momentum for the study, had provided the financial resources, and brought international expertise in work of this type. The MoEYS was involved because the study was a form of capacity-building and sensitisation for government personnel, and because the study could benefit from the MoEYS infrastructure at the national, provincial and local levels. In 2004 the work was contracted to a consultancy firm headed by the second-named author (Seng Bunly), which conducted the work with advice from the first-named author (Mark Bray). The MoEYS gave its full cooperation to the work, and provided letters of introduction and authorisation to provincial and local officials.

In the field itself, the following data collection techniques were used:

- *School surveys:* School directors and teachers completed the questionnaires, with assistance from enumerators who helped to check relevant documents. Different questionnaires were used for primary and secondary schools, and a checklist was used when collecting information from pupils. Supplementary information was obtained from school committees, but the majority of committee members were poorly informed about costs. Data from the pupils were used to cross-check the data from the school directors and teachers.

- *Focus group discussions:* Four focus group discussions were conducted in each focus site. These groups were primary teachers, secondary teachers, parents, and lower secondary pupils. The views of primary pupils were not sought in the focus group discussions since these pupils were generally considered to be too young to provide useful information on costs. The discussions focused mainly on the private costs of basic education and on perceptions of the PAP and the government's recently-introduced scholarship programme.

- *In-depth interviews with pupils for information validation:* Focus group discussions provided general information on quantities and prices of goods consumed by the pupils. In order to get detailed information on household costs by grade, individual interviews with pupils were conducted to validate the information of focus group discussions and obtain detailed information on specific items.

- *Market check*: The prices of different items were cross-checked with those in the market in each focus site.

Assumptions and Weights

As expected, the research team found that expenditures varied according to each family's standard of living, with the poor paying little and the rich paying more. In view of this, weighted averages were used in the final calculation. For example, one question was: "In this school, what percentage of pupils have bicycles, and what percentage do not?". This permitted weighting of the cost of bicycles according to the proportion of children who actually had bicycles. Of course the proportion was not a precise figure; and some students who had bicycles may not have used them to come to school because they lived next door to the school. Nevertheless, the weighted calculation was felt to provide a more accurate portrait than raw figures.

The example of the bicycle can also illustrate a different dimension in the estimation, namely the rate of depreciation. The team devoted some effort to determining the life-span of a bicycle under different conditions. In general, bicycles in Cambodia are used intensively:

they commonly carry more than one person at a time, and they are used over rough terrain. Also, young people are usually less caring about their bicycles than are mature adults. However, estimation of an average life-span is not easy because of the variations in ways that bicycles can be treated and because parts can be replaced as necessary. In view of these considerations, the final assumption on which this research is based is that bicycles have life-spans of six years. Along similar lines, the life-spans of motorbikes (used by some lower secondary pupils themselves, as well as by their family members to deliver the students to school) were estimated at eight years.

Since some expenses were incurred daily or weekly, another question for the research concerned the number of days and weeks in a school year. The calculations which follow are based on the assumption of a school year with nine months (12 months minus 2.5 months for summer vacation and 0.5 months for Khmer New Year holidays). The primary school calendar is taken to have 180 days per year (i.e. five days per week), whereas the lower secondary school calendar is taken to have 216 days per year (i.e. six days per week). Again, recognition that pupils are not at school all day, every day requires estimates of use of bicycles etc. to be adjusted for non-school periods.

A further question concerned the school tests, since the fees that are commonly charged for tests, especially in lower secondary schools, become a major household cost. The calculations which follow assume that lower secondary schools operate monthly tests for five months in each school year, of which three months are in the first semester and two months are in the second semester. In addition, at the end of each semester is an examination.

Some further balances had to be reached when, for example, pupils, teachers and parents all produced different estimates of the costs of particular items. In these cases, the enumerators discussed the differences and sought consensus on the appropriate estimates to use. When aggregating data, the research team then made further adjustments to allow for the different prices in urban, rural and remote areas.

Most of the data from the survey which follow, therefore, are estimated averages for the pupils of specific grades in specific schools. The data do not show ranges within those grades, e.g. for children of rich and poor households; and the research has made assumptions about the extent to which the sampled schools may be considered typical of the country as a whole. However, the analysis of the survey data has been undertaken in the context of other available research. Some of this research does show variations in expenditures according to different income groups. Other studies (e.g. Sokha & Seng 2000; Keng 2004a) also provide data on specific features in specific communities, and therefore help show some of the variations around the country.

Household Costs

The main part of this section on household costs focuses on data from the 2004 survey, which are presented in eight categories. Some costs are mostly incurred at the beginning of the school year, while others are incurred during the year. The eight categories are registration and record books; uniforms and equipment; learning materials; supplementary tutoring; tests and examinations; transport; pocket money; and other expenses. The second part of the section compares these findings with data from the government's socio-economic surveys and other sources. In the tables that follow, the urban category includes semi-urban schools, and the rural category includes remote schools.

Data from the 2004 Survey

Registration and Record Books

Prior to the launch of the PAP, schools commonly charged parents for registration. In 1997/98, 14 of the 77 primary schools surveyed imposed registration charges in Grade 1, ranging from 200 to 2,500 riels per pupil and averaging 1,000 riels (Bray 1999a, p.49). According to informal evidence, at the secondary level charges were commonly about 10 times that figure, i.e. in the region of 10,000 riels. With the launch of the PAP, such charges, together with other obligatory contributions of various kinds, were prohibited. This prohibition was given strong publicity throughout the country, and was a major factor in the jumps in primary school enrolment during 2000, 2001 and 2002. The authorities deserve considerable credit for these outcomes. Some schools did still find ways to impose some charges. For example, if pupils did not complete the forms correctly, fees of 200 to 500 riels might be demanded. Also, in some areas pupils asked the teachers to fill out the forms and paid about 500 riels for the service. However, these payments were the exception rather than the norm.

The contributions which had previously been demanded were in effect fees under a different name. In 1997/98, contributions were demanded in all except six of the 77 primary schools surveyed (Bray 1999a, p.49). Five of these six schools were in rural parts of Ratanakiri, which was sparsely populated and had a less monetised economy than many other regions of the country. The sixth school, in Takeo, had decided to seek other ways to raise revenue but was being forced to consider reintroduction of per-pupil contributions. The average per-pupil contribution for the 77 schools was 2,500 riels. Among provinces with more than two schools sampled, average charges in Ratanakiri were by far the lowest (300 riels) while those in Banteay Meanchey were the highest (4,550 riels). This appeared to reflect general income levels in those provinces. Survey data for lower secondary schools in 1997/98 were not available, but the level of contributions was considerably greater than that for primary schools. The 2004 survey did find evidence of a few persisting contributions in both primary and lower secondary schools, but they were only in the region of 200 to 500 riels and in general the government policy appeared to have been successful in replacing these household costs with the PAP.

Similar remarks apply to the monthly and yearly record books, which recorded the pupils' scores along with progress reports, and had spaces for comments from the parents and teachers. The 2004 survey indicated that in all schools the record books themselves were provided free of charge in accordance with MoEYS regulations. In a few cases, parents paid the teachers 500 riels to fill in the books, and pupils in some schools were required to purchase covers. However, such practices were not the norm.

Schools in Phnom Penh required photographs for the monthly record books, and many schools both in Phnom Penh and elsewhere also required photographs for identity cards. These photographs were not demanded in all schools and or all grades: much depended on decisions at the institutional level. Photographs were more costly in rural and remote areas than in semi-urban or urban areas, and typically cost 1,500 to 2,500 riels.

Table 8 summarises the survey data on registration and related costs. Figures have been averaged, to reflect the proportions of pupils required to make payments in each category. The jump in costs in Grade 3 (urban) and Grade 4 (rural) chiefly reflects the demands for photographs. Although photographs cost more in rural areas than in urban areas – and even more in remote areas – not all rural pupils were required to supply the photographs, and the average figure was therefore less than in the urban areas. In general, costs were higher in urban areas, though these areas also had higher incomes. As anticipated, registration and related costs were generally greater in lower secondary than in primary schools.

Table 8: Summary of Per-Pupil Costs of Registration and Record Books, by Grade and Region (Riels)

	Urban	Rural
Grade 1	200	100
Grade 2	200	100
Grade 3	2,500	200
Grade 4	900	1,400
Grade 5	400	200
Grade 6	2,500	2,300
Grade 7	4,500	2,600
Grade 8	2,600	800
Grade 9	2,700	900

Uniforms and Equipment

Most schools in Cambodia require pupils to wear uniforms, though the requirement is enforced less strictly in primary than in secondary schools, and less strictly in rural and remote areas than in urban areas. The number of uniforms used per year varies by individual, by socio-economic group, and by region. Pupils in poor families commonly have only one uniform or none at all, but pupils from medium-income and prosperous families commonly have two new uniforms every year.

Since pupils would always require some clothes, it is arguable that only the extra expenses of a uniform compared with other clothes should be considered a cost of schooling. The cost of uniforms increases as pupils get older and need larger clothes, and prices of course also depend on quality. A new uniform required between 14,000 and 20,000 riels and a second-hand one cost 4,000 to 6,000 riels. In remote areas, the price was higher than in rural and urban areas. For the calculations below, only 70 per cent of the price was taken as a cost of schooling, on the grounds that children would always need some sort of clothing whether or not they were in school.

Similar remarks apply to shoes. Poor children may not wear shoes out of school, but they were expected to wear shoes in school and usually did so. In general, pupils used two or three pairs of shoes every year, though poor pupils used only one pair of shoes. The price of shoes varied according to quality and size. The most simple pair cost 1,500 to 2,500 riels, depending on size, and then went up to 8,000 riels for better quality.

In addition, sports kits are mandatory in urban and in semi-urban areas. Since sports kits would not be required for children not in school, they are entirely an expense arising from enrolment in school. The price of sports kits ranged from 4,000 riels to 10,000 riels according to quality and brand, with additional expenditures needed for sports shoes. Many schools permitted students to wear their uniforms for sports if they were unable to purchase kits.

Finally, most primary pupils use satchels to hold their learning materials and stationery. A cheap satchel cost 1,500 riels, and an expensive one cost 12,000 riels. Most pupils use satchels for about three years, but some pupils change their satchels every year. Pupils who either cannot afford or do not wish to use satchels use plastic bags which do not cost anything. Lower secondary pupils, in particular, put their notebooks in plastic bags and carry them around in their bicycle baskets. In lower secondary school, fewer pupils use satchels than at primary school. About a quarter of pupils do not use satchels, especially boys.

Table 9 summarises uniform and equipment costs, discounting for the fact that pupils would need some clothing whether or not they were in school and averaging out costs for the proportion of pupils who do not purchase sports kits. Pupils in rural areas were not expected to make so many purchases as their counterparts in urban areas. The same applied to pupils in remote schools, but for them the unit costs were particularly high.

Table 9: Summary of Per-Pupil Costs of Uniforms and Equipment, by Grade and Region (Riels)

	Urban	Rural
Grade 1	16,900	11,700
Grade 2	17,100	12,000
Grade 3	17,600	12,700
Grade 4	21,300	16,000
Grade 5	21,900	16,700
Grade 6	23,900	17,100
Grade 7	42,300	25,800
Grade 8	42,300	26,700
Grade 9	42,600	26,700

Note: The component for uniforms has been discounted by 30% on the grounds that children would have to be clothed whether or not they were in school.

Learning Materials

During the 1990s, the government launched a scheme through which both primary and secondary pupils could borrow textbooks without charge. The scheme was then expanded under the PAP 7 (MoEYS 2003, p.61). The survey found that this scheme was generally working as intended, and therefore that households did not need to make significant investments for textbooks. Some pupils in Phnom Penh were still expected to purchase books, but the scheme had reached semi-urban and rural areas as intended. The scheme relieved households of annual expenditures of about 16,000 riels per primary pupil and 28,000 riels per lower secondary pupil.

As a result, the remaining expenditures for textbooks were minor. Pupils were normally asked to buy covers at a cost of 100 to 200 riels each. Pupils in most primary grades needed four textbooks, and their secondary school counterparts needed about seven; but a shortage of books commonly required pairs of lower secondary students to share sets of books, which allowed them to share the cost of covers. Lost books had to be replaced at the pupils' expense, which required about 3,500 to 4,000 riels per book.

Households also needed to purchase various learning materials. Some expenditures were incurred as the year progressed, but the large expenditures were at the beginning of the school year. These were as follows:

- *Notebooks:* Expenditure on notebooks depended on the numbers and types of notebooks. Grade 1 demanded only three notebooks, but Grade 9 demanded about 24 notebooks. Some poor students reduced the number of notebooks purchased. The price of notebooks was generally in the range 500 to 900 riels, depending on the quality and the number of pages, with little variation in prices in different locations.
- *Exercise books:* No exercise books were required from Grades 1 to 3. Exercise books were available for Grades 4 to 9 in the market, but only a few primary pupils had them. Pupils needed more exercise books in Grade 9 when they prepared for upper secondary education. In the Kampot schools visited, teachers prohibited pupils from bringing exercise books to class, because the teachers used the materials from the exercise books for classwork. Some pupils purchased the exercise books for supplementary use, and gained help to understand the materials during the private tuition classes. The price of exercise books was between 1,500 and 2,500 riels, depending on size and publisher.
- *Other stationery:* Pupils needed pens, pencils, rubbers, rulers and other stationery. The expenditure on these materials depended on grades, socio-economic groups, and the behaviour of pupils. Poor pupils had only pieces of chalk, boards and pencils in their satchels, whereas rich pupils had higher-cost materials such as crayons. Some parents complained that their children used a lot of learning materials, such as a pencil every week.

Table 10 summarises these expenditures and shows variations by grade. The range in urban areas is from 7,700 riels in Grade 1 to 36,300 riels in Grade 9. Rural pupils consumed lower quantities and inferior quality learning materials. The highest expenditures were in urban areas, but costs in remote areas were slightly higher than in rural areas.

Table 10: Summary of Per-Pupil Costs of Learning Materials, by Grade and Region (Riels)

	Urban	Rural
Grade 1	7,700	5,000
Grade 2	9,600	6,200
Grade 3	12,100	8,700
Grade 4	15,400	10,300
Grade 5	17,300	12,200
Grade 6	20,000	14,400
Grade 7	27,100	17,500
Grade 8	31,000	19,900
Grade 9	36,300	24,500

Supplementary Tutoring

Many households pay for tutoring to supplement the standard classes. Supplementary tutoring, which operates as a sort of shadow system alongside the mainstream (Bray 1999b), consumes considerable household resources, especially in urban areas. Expenditures vary from one grade to another, peaking in primary school at Grade 6 and in lower secondary school at Grade 9. Some rural primary schools have no tutoring in Grades 1 to 5 but only in Grade 6, that being especially important as the final grade of primary school and as a determinant of entry to lower secondary school.

From the supply side, private tutoring may be classified in two categories. First, teachers provide extra classes for their own pupils, often in the same classrooms as for the mainstream lessons. This mechanism provides extra incomes for teachers, and extends exposure to the materials in the official curriculum, but may involve an element of blackmail. Pupils may find that they have little choice over whether or not to join the supplementary classes, especially when the teachers decide which pupils pass the end-of-year examinations and are promoted to the next class. In the second category, teachers provide supplementary classes to pupils for whom they are not already responsible.

These classes may be in the schools in which the teachers are already employed, or they may be in other schools, the teachers' homes, the pupils' homes, or other locations. Groups may be large or small, depending on supply and demand.

When households conduct informal cost-benefit analyses, they may decide that investment in supplementary tutoring is a wise use of resources to avoid negative consequences. Thus refusal to pay for tutoring may cause the child to have to repeat a grade, which would then cost more than the tutoring. Peer pressure also plays a role: neither pupils nor families like to feel left behind in something that is being received by everybody else.

In Phnom Penh, supplementary tutoring has become blurred with mainstream classes. Thus, teachers commonly charge 300 riels to 500 riels per day for regular classes, and then include all students in whatever lessons are provided. However, even these teachers may provide extra lessons on specified days each week. Such classes typically cost 400 riels per pupil for each two-hour class.

In some semi-urban areas, teachers charge 200 to 300 riels per pupil for such classes, but not all teachers and classes operate in this system. In the semi-urban school in Kampot that was included in the survey, the proportions of pupils receiving tutoring were as follows:

Grade 1	0%
Grade 2	0%
Grade 3	25-40%
Grade 4	40-60%
Grade 5	50-75%
Grade 6	60-80%

Whereas in primary school the tutoring usually covers the whole curriculum, in lower secondary school it is specialised by subject. The four most popular subjects are mathematics, physics, chemistry and Khmer literature, and in urban areas many pupils take classes in English. Some pupils receive tutoring from their own teachers, and some receive it from different teachers. The cost of tutoring varies not only by location but also by subject. The fees for mathematics and physics are about 500 riels per hour in urban areas, and 300 to 400 riels in rural areas. The fees for other subjects are lower. In Phnom Penh, pupils commonly receive private lessons six days a week for mathematics, physics and chemistry, but only attend Khmer literature classes one or two days a week.

Table 11 summarises the data on costs of supplementary tutoring. The table shows tutoring costs from Grade 1 onwards in the urban sample but only from Grade 6 onwards in the rural sample. Tutoring costs at the lower secondary level were also much higher in the urban than the rural sample.

Table 11: Summary of Per-Pupil Costs of Supplementary Tutoring, by Grade and Region (Riels)

	Urban	Rural
Grade 1	21,100	0
Grade 2	21,500	0
Grade 3	32,600	0
Grade 4	38,100	0
Grade 5	40,700	0
Grade 6	48,700	3,300
Grade 7	66,000	15,300
Grade 8	81,700	17,100
Grade 9	211,400	63,500

Tests and Examinations

In the past, households spent considerable amounts on tests and examinations. Some expenditures are still incurred, but they have been much reduced by the PAP.

The costs of tests and examinations include both the necessary materials and the fees charged by the MoEYS. Registration for lower secondary school examinations and expenditures on photographs are included in the calculations. During the academic year, most schools hold both monthly tests and semester examinations. Three monthly tests are held in the first semester, and are followed by an end-of-semester examination; and two monthly tests are held in the second semester and are followed by a second end-of-semester examination. Most teachers allow pupils to use paper from their notebooks to write the tests. However, some teachers sell monthly test papers at about 200 riels per page, in which case households may spend approximately 2,200 per month on tests. In addition, at the end of Grade 9, lower secondary school pupils must pay an examination fee set by the MoEYS. This fee is 3,000 to 3,500 riels per pupil. After the introduction of the PAP, teachers were prohibited from charging for monthly test papers. In some provinces, the rule was applied strictly but in other provinces some payments were still collected.

Table 12 summarises data from the survey on average expenditures on examinations. At the primary level, very few costs were incurred. However in urban lower secondary schools, expenditures ranged from 15,200 riels in Grade 7 to 21,300 riels in Grade 9.

Table 12: Summary of Per-Pupil Costs of Tests and Examinations, by Grade and Region (Riels)

	Urban	Rural
Grade 1	100	0
Grade 2	100	0
Grade 3	800	0
Grade 4	800	0
Grade 5	800	0
Grade 6	900	0
Grade 7	15,200	2,100
Grade 8	15,200	2,100
Grade 9	21,300	9,100

Transport

Throughout Cambodia, pupils use bicycles as the main means of transport. Very young children either walk to school or are transported by their parents, but pupils commonly start riding their own bicycles in Grade 3. The survey found that above that grade between 20 and 80 per cent of primary pupils and between 40 and 80 per cent of lower secondary pupils owned bicycles. Parents sometimes deliver children to school by motorbike; and in upper secondary school (though less commonly in lower secondary school) pupils may themselves drive motorbikes.

The costs of maintaining and repairing bicycles vary by region, by use and by gender. Poor roads in remote and rural areas create higher costs than in urban and semi-urban areas; and boys tend to treat their bicycles more roughly than girls. With these factors in mind, annual costs for maintenance and repairs have been averaged at 25,000 to 30,000 riels.

In rural areas, few pupils use moto-taxis[1] or minibuses for school transportation, though pupils in one school visited in Battambang had to pay 200 riels per day for ferry crossings. Only in Phnom Penh are minibuses commonly used by pupils. In Bak Touk School, about 10 per cent of pupils regularly used minibuses at an approximate monthly cost of 40,000 riels. In urban areas, even some pupils in the lowest grades incurred some transport costs.

Table 13 summarises the costs of transport, allowing for the fact that bicycles etc. would not be used only for travelling to and from school. Costs were highest in urban areas in all grades. In Phnom Penh, pupils had to pay not only for initial purchase and maintenance of bicycles but also for daily parking. In Bak Touk school, for example, Grade 6 pupils had to pay an average of 7,200 riels per annum for parking, and Grade 9 pupils paid as much as 43,600 riels.

Table 13: Summary of Per-Pupil Costs of Transport, by Grade and Region (Riels)

	Urban	Rural
Grade 1	11,200	0
Grade 2	11,200	0
Grade 3	18,500	5,400
Grade 4	25,500	12,900
Grade 5	28,600	19,000
Grade 6	33,000	23,100
Grade 7	37,400	35,000
Grade 8	37,500	35,000
Grade 9	37,900	35,000

Pocket Money

Most parents give children pocket money for snacks and breakfast. Where the school is far from home, children may also receive money for lunch. Expenditures vary considerably among different socio-

---

[1] i.e. motorbikes being used as taxis.

economic groups, and some rich families provide extra money for entertainment and other activities not related to education.

As with uniforms, the question arises whether pocket money should be considered a cost of schooling. Just as children need to be clothed whether or not they are in school, children need to eat whether or not they are in school. Parents clearly considered pocket money to be a cost of schooling; and when pupils purchased food, the cost was usually higher than if the pupils had eaten at home. Balancing these factors, raw data on expenditures were discounted by 30 per cent.

The survey found that parents in semi-urban areas usually gave their children 200 to 500 riels per day in Grades 1 to 3, and 500 to 1,000 riels in Grades 4 to 6. In Phnom Penh, standard amounts were between 500 and 2,000 riels per pupil per day. In rural areas, amounts were usually 100 to 300 riels in Grades 1 to 3, and 200 to 500 riels in Grades 4 to 6. Some poor families did not give pocket money to children, so the children tried to earn their own money for school.

In some primary schools, the WFP operates a school-feeding programme which is targeted on poor rural communities. This programme, which was launched on a pilot basis in 1999 and then expanded, aims not only to improve pupils' nutrition but also to give them sufficiently full stomachs to permit them to concentrate on learning. During survey design, it had been anticipated that pupils in receipt of food from the WFP would receive smaller amounts of pocket money from their parents. However, this correlation was not found. For example, in Chambak Primary School, Takeo Province, amounts of pocket money were as high as in other rural schools which did not receive WFP assistance. One reason may be that the WFP targeting of poor communities was not sufficiently accurate. Another reason may be that children still purchased their own snacks because they were bored with the standard diet of the WFP scheme.

As indicated in Table 14, the costs of pocket money continued to rise through the grades of lower secondary schooling. As with some other items, the costs in remote areas were sometimes greater than in rural areas. In many households, pocket money was the largest single item of expenditure, though urban households with secondary pupils commonly paid more for tutoring.

While these expenditures were generally gender-neutral, the survey found that some parents in Phnom Penh provided more money to boys than to girls. This allowed the boys to spend more money on games and other activities.

Table 14: Summary of Per-Pupil Costs of Pocket Money, by Grade and Region (Riels)

	Urban	Rural
Grade 1	57,900	25,400
Grade 2	60,300	27,700
Grade 3	61,800	28,400
Grade 4	68,300	41,700
Grade 5	76,000	44,000
Grade 6	82,300	46,300
Grade 7	182,900	91,100
Grade 8	190,400	96,900
Grade 9	203,500	113,400

Note: These figures have been discounted by 30% on the grounds that much expenditure from pocket money is on food, and children would have to eat whether or not they were in school.

Other Expenses

Pupils do incur other expenses from time to time during the year (Table 15). These include gifts to teachers, collections during festivals, and ceremonies of various kinds. For example, schools usually collect money for female teachers during Women's Day, March 8. Contributions are not obligatory, but pupils commonly pay 200 to 500 riels each. Some schools also collect money for the Khmer New Year ceremony. In urban areas, these collections may reach 5,000 riels per pupil.

Schools which are linked to pagodas may also raise funds for religious ceremonies. Such contributions commonly range from 100 riels to 500 riels. Parents may also be asked to contribute labour and materials to construction and maintenance of facilities.

In addition, pupils in remote areas may also have to board on an informal basis. Formal boarding did exist in some schools during earlier eras, but was phased out by the MoEYS in the late 1980s and early 1990s. Most informal boarding that remained was in the pagodas, which mainly served boys rather than girls. Some primary schools are incomplete in the sense of not having all grades. Children who are old enough then have to travel further for schooling. These factors push up the costs for rural and remote schools, though Table 15 still shows that overall expenses were higher in urban (including semi-urban) areas.

Table 15: Summary of Other Per-Pupil Costs, by Grade and Region (Riels)

	Urban	Rural
Grade 1	1,900	400
Grade 2	1,900	400
Grade 3	2,000	600
Grade 4	2,100	700
Grade 5	2,100	700
Grade 6	2,900	700
Grade 7	3,800	1,900
Grade 8	3,800	2,000
Grade 9	3,800	2,100

Summary

Tables 16 and 17 compile the data from Tables 8 to 15 to provide a con-solidated list of direct household costs per year for schooling at primary and lower levels. In addition to these direct costs, of course, are indirect (opportunity) costs, which are considered below.

Expenditure patterns vary by region, with supplementary provide tutoring being more significant in urban areas than in rural aras, particu-larly at the primary level. However, pocket money and transport are consistently most prominent in primary schooling (except in urban ar-eas, where tutoring comes second), which pocket money and tutoring are the largest items in secondary education.

As anticipated, the consolidated tables show that in all locations costs increase with the grades. However, costs in rural primary schools are only 30 to 45 per cent of those in urban schools, with the proportion increasing in the higher grades. A similar pattern is evident at lower secondary education. The cost of Grade 7 jumps significantly from that in Grade 6, and costs continue to grow as the grades increase. Supple-mentary tutoring becomes even more important than in primary, and the costs of pocket money also escalate.

Table 16: Direct Per-Pupil Costs of Primary Schooling Incurred by Households (Riels)

	Grade 1	Grade 2	Grade 3	Grade 4	Grade 5	Grade 6
Urban Areas						
Registration and record books	200	200	2,500	900	400	2,500
Uniforms and equipment	16,900	17,100	17,600	21,300	21,900	23,900
Learning materials	7,700	9,600	12,100	15,400	17,300	20,000
Supplementary tutoring	21,000	21,500	32,600	38,100	40,700	48,700
Tests and examinations	100	100	800	800	800	900
Transport	11,200	11,200	18,500	25,500	28,600	33,000
Pocket money	57,900	60,300	61,800	68,300	76,000	82,300
Other expenses	1,900	1,900	2,000	2,100	2,200	2,900
Total	*116,900*	*121,980*	*147,900*	*172,500*	*187,900*	*214,200*
Rural Areas						
Registration and record books	100	100	200	1,400	200	2,300
Uniforms and equipment	11,700	12,000	12,700	16,000	16,700	17,100
Learning materials	5,000	6,200	8,700	10,300	12,200	14,400
Supplementary tutoring	0	0	0	0	0	3,300
Tests and examinations	0	0	0	0	0	0
Transport	0	0	5,400	12,900	19,000	23,100
Pocket money	25,400	27,700	28,400	41,700	44,000	46,300
Other expenses	400	400	600	700	700	700
Total	*42,500*	*46,200*	*56,000*	*83,200*	*91,900*	*107,200*

Since exactly the same set of primary schools were surveyed in 1997/98 and in 2004, it is possible to make comparisons over time. These comparisons must be treated with caution because of inconsistencies in the data despite efforts to use similar methods of data collection. Nevertheless, Table 18 shows a dramatic reduction of household costs in every grade between 1997/98 and 2004. On average, household costs at Grade 1 in 2004 were only 36.9 per cent of their 1997/98 level, and the figure for Grade 6 was 46.3 per cent. Furthermore, in real terms the reduction was even more marked. The data in Table 18 show costs at current prices. According to the National Institute of Statistics (2004), in urban areas the consumer price index between 2000 and 2003 rose at approximately 2.0 per cent per annum. Application of this proportion to the figures in Table 18 would mean that at 1997/98 prices the average Grade 1 cost would be only 74,100 riels and therefore that the 2004 figure would be only 33.4 per cent of the 1997/98 one. For Grade 6, the cost would be 168,500 riels, representing only 41.8 per cent of the 1997/98 one. This decrease in household costs has chiefly been achieved through the PAP, which significantly reduced the direct costs on households, chiefly by reducing (and in some cases almost entirely removing) the demands for registration, learning materials and tests.

Table 17: Direct Per-Pupil Household Costs of Lower Secondary Schooling Incurred by Households (Riels)

	Grade 7	Grade 8	Grade 9
Urban Areas			
Registration and record books	4,500	2,600	2,700
Uniforms and equipment	42,300	42,300	42,600
Learning materials	27,100	31,000	36,300
Supplementary tutoring	66,000	81,700	211,400
Tests and examinations	15,200	15,200	21,300
Transport	37,400	37,500	37,900
Pocket money	182,900	190,400	203,500
Other expenses	3,800	3,800	3,800
Total	*379,300*	*402,700*	*559,500*
Rural Areas			
Registration and record books	2,600	800	900
Uniforms and equipment	25,800	26,700	26,700
Learning materials	17,500	19,900	24,500
Supplementary tutoring	15,300	17,100	63,500
Tests and examinations	2,100	2,100	9,100
Transport	35,000	35,000	35,000
Pocket money	91,100	96,900	113,400
Other expenses	1,900	2,000	2,100
Total	*191,300*	*200,600*	*275,200*

Comparative Data from Previous Surveys

This set of findings can also be usefully places alongside data from other surveys. One set of data was produced by the Ministry of Planning's 2000 Cambodia Poverty Assessment, which was itself based on the 1997 Socio-Economic Survey. Once again, the survey had sampling and other limitations which must be taken into account (Council for Social Development 2002), but the data are useful because they group household expenditures on education by overall household expenditure quintiles. The 1997 Socio-Economic Survey covered 6,010 households in 474 villages and 21 provinces.

Table 19 shows first that enrolment rates differed substantially in the different expenditure quintiles. This was especially marked at the level of lower secondary education, in which the richest quintiles had enrolment rates of 31.0 per cent compared with just 5.6 per cent in the poorest quintiles.

Table 18: Household Per-Pupil Costs of Primary Schooling, by Province and Grade, 1997/98 and 2004 (Riels, at Current Prices)

Province/Municipality	Year	Grade 1	Grade 2	Grade 3
Banteay Meanchey	1997/98	362,400	362,400	438,200
	2004	81,500	83,600	87,200
Battambang	1997/98	303,300	296,200	307,600
	2004	61,000	61,700	82,800
Kampot	1997/98	62,600	71,100	119,000
	2004	50,400	52,360	129,700
Phnom Penh	1997/98	396,500	621,500	654,600
	2004	200,300	204,500	254,000
Ratanakiri	1997/98	154,600	154,600	88,500
	2004	66,400	70,500	84,900
Svay Rieng	1997/98	215,900	217,500	219,500
	2004	67,400	74,645	90,300
Takeo	1997/98	59,500	66,800	76,700
	2004	47,000	52,100	66,800
Average	**1997/98**	**222,100**	**255,700**	**271,900**
	2004	**82,000**	**85,600**	**113,700**

Province/Municipality	Year	Grade 4	Grade 5	Grade 6
Banteay Meanchey	1997/98	497,000	505,600	531,100
	2004	120,500	129,600	156,200
Battambang	1997/98	350,300	384,000	479,200
	2004	117,500	130,600	144,000
Kampot	1997/98	139,000	154,100	169,500
	2004	106,800	115,200	137,900
Phnom Penh	1997/98	546,100	627,800	709,600
	2004	262,600	282,300	310,200
Ratanakiri	1997/98	187,600	187,600	243,800
	2004	113,500	127,900	282,000
Svay Rieng	1997/98	275,100	322,700	313,600
	2004	114,900	129,000	146,000
Takeo	1997/98	104,600	391,000	374,000
	2004	97,200	107,800	128,200
Average	**1997/98**	**299,900**	**367,500**	**403,000**
	2004	**133,300**	**146,100**	**186,400**

Note: The figures for 1997/98 are taken from Bray (1999a), pp.121-125. They have been adjusted by discounting expenditures on uniforms and pocket money by 30%, to match the parallel discount in the 2004 data. Also, the 1997/98 figure for Grade 5 in Phnom Penh has been adjusted to allow for sampling bias.

These enrolment rates to a large extent reflected the costs of schooling relative to household incomes. Thus in the poorest households, the average schooling expenditures per primary school child would have consumed 26.2 per cent of non-food spending. These figures are not entirely straightforward, because they refer to average expenditures across all quintiles, and presumably the poorest families spent less per child than the richest families. Nevertheless, it is clear that families with several children in school would have faced a very severe burden. Indeed a household in the poorest quintile which spent the average per child and had four children in school would have found that all its non-food expenditure would have been consumed by schooling. By contrast, in the richest household the average schooling expenditure per primary school child would have consumed 11.9 per cent of household non-food spending. At lower secondary education, the range was 56.9 per cent in the lowest quintile to 26.2 per cent in the highest quintile. Although the proportions in the highest quintile were much lower than in other quintiles, the proportions were still considerable, especially for families which had more than one child in school. Such figures gave further impetus to the reforms launched in 2000.

Elaborating on these statistics, Figures 3 and 4 are a pair of pie charts on expenditures on education for the poorest and the richest quintiles. The size of the pie charts reflects the fact that total reported annual expenditures per primary student were four and half times greater for the richest quintile than for the poorest quintile. Private tutoring costs comprised 19 per cent of all primary expenditures for the richest households, compared to only 1 per cent for the poorest. In contrast, school fees accounted for 12 per cent of poor household primary education expenditure but only 5 per cent for the richest households.

Table 19: Enrolment Rates and Education Affordability Ratios, by Expenditure Quintiles, 1997

	Expenditure Quintiles				
	1 (poorest)	2	3	4	5 (richest)
Net enrolment rates					
Primary	55.4	64.7	70.5	73.2	77.5
Lower Secondary	5.6	6.0	13.0	17.1	31.0
Ratio of average schooling expenditure per student to household non-food spending					
Primary	26.2	21.0	18.9	17.7	11.9
Lower Secondary	56.9	50.2	41.5	34.0	26.2

Source: 2000 Cambodia Poverty Assessment, quoted in Ondrusek (2002), p.9.

Figure 3: Household Expenditures on Primary Education, Poorest Quintile, 1997

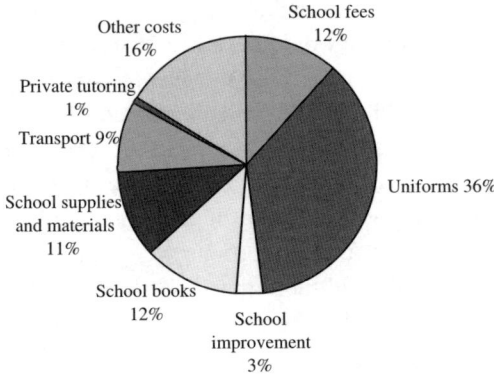

Source: 2000 Cambodia Poverty Assessment, reproduced in Ondrusek (2002), p.11.

Figure 4: Household Expenditures on Primary Education, Richest Quintile, 1997

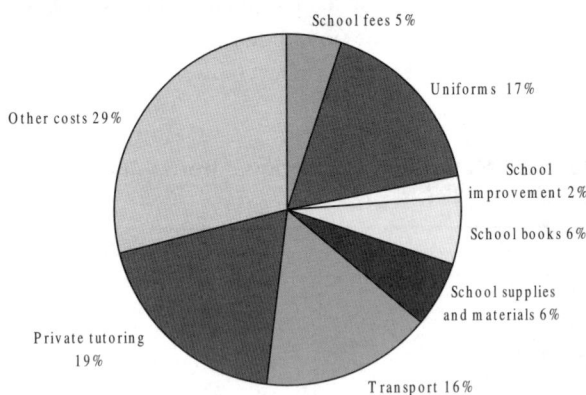

Source: 2000 Cambodia Poverty Assessment, reproduced in Ondrusek (2002), p.11.

Another useful set of statistics was provided in 2001 by the NGO Kampuchean Action for Primary Education (KAPE). The costs of lower secondary schooling for girls were estimated in order to design a scholarship scheme in Kampong Cham Province (MoEYS & KAPE 2001, pp.12-13; Velasco 2004, p.47). The estimated costs, reproduced in Table 20, did not allow for snacks for children who lived close to the school, but did allow for lunch money for children who lived 10-14 kilometres from the school, and boarding for those who lived 15 or more kilometres away. KAPE stressed that these costs detailed what was required for "successful" completion of lower secondary education by girls from poor backgrounds. In this respect, while tutoring and study paper fees charged by teachers might have seemed optional, in fact they were not because those who did not pay often failed.

Table 20: Estimated Annual Costs of Lower Secondary Schooling, Kampong Cham Province, 2001

	Cost (US$)	Category 1 Girls less than 10 km from school	Category 2 Girls 10-14 km from school	Category 3 Girls 15 or more km from school
Bicycle*	43.00	x	x	x
Bicycle lock*	1.00	x	x	x
Educational supplies	1.00	x	x	x
Study paper fees	8.20	x	x	x
Parking fees for bicycle	8.00	x	x	x
Uniform (2 sets)	10.00	x	x	x
Tutoring fees	7.00	x	x	x
Copy books	9.80	x	x	x
Pens	0.90	x	x	x
Lunch money	40.00		x	
Boarding costs (8.5 months)	114.75			x
Room costs (8.5 months)	42.5			x
Total	---	88.90	128.90	246.15

* capital cost, needed only in the first year of study

Source: MoEYS & KAPE (2001), p.13.

Opportunity Costs

Two different types of opportunity costs are identified in the literature (see e.g. Cohn & Geske 1990; Tsang 1997; Wang 2001). First is the lost utility from the fact that expenditures on school-related items cannot be deployed to other uses; and second is the lost income from a child's schooling which arises because the child cannot work elsewhere when in school or travelling to/from school. Both types of opportunity cost are difficult to calculate, especially because they depend on arbitrary assumptions not only about economic values but also about individual preferences. Nevertheless, at least some general statements can be made.

Although no efforts have been made to measure the first type of opportunity cost in Cambodia, light is shed on the matter by research in other settings. In China, for example, Wang (2001) calculated the direct costs of both primary and lower secondary education, and noted the alternative uses of such sums in fertilisers and pesticides. He then observed that many families could not afford sufficient fertilisers and pesticides, from which he concluded that the agricultural yields of these families would have been larger if they had not invested in schooling. Similar judgements could no doubt be made in Cambodia, and would provide one estimate of the opportunity costs of households' direct expenditures on education. Such costs are of greatest significance to the poorest families.

Concerning the second type of opportunity cost, i.e. of income foregone, some research has been conducted in Cambodia; and again lessons may be learned from research in other settings. Two general statements provide starting points. First, opportunity costs may be different for boys and girls: boys commonly earn higher incomes in formal employment, but in domestic work, including the care of younger siblings, girls may provide an important role in releasing adults for external employment. Second, opportunity costs increase as children grow older.

The question what the households whose children attended school had to forego because their children attended school is less abstract in Cambodia than it would be in many other countries because many children indeed do not attend school and do make economic contributions to the welfare of their families (UNDP 2000; Gourley 2000). During the workshops for the 1997/98 study (Bray 1999a, p.63), parents estimated that a boy who worked in a provincial town on a construction site might earn 3,000 riels a day, 15 days a month and five months a year. This would give an annual income of 225,000 riels. Alternatively, a girl might be hired to transplant and harvest rice. The income from this would be 2,000 riels a day for 70 days, i.e. about 140,000 riels during both rainy and dry seasons. Additional income could be raised from pig-raising and scarf-weaving, for example, though this element may be discounted since children who do attend school are still available to help their families outside school hours. The value of inputs of children who worked directly for their families without remuneration may be taken as comparable to those who were paid to work. As in other countries (see e.g. Zoungrana et al. 1997, p.13; Colclough et al. 2000, p.7; Rose & Al-Samarrai 2001, p.41; UNESCO 2003, p.119), girls were more likely to be withdrawn from school because they were perceived to be more suited to domestic duties. Girls were more likely than boys to assist their mothers in bringing up siblings and attending to household chores such as fetching water.

Gender differences were also evident in the findings of a 1998 national survey of 1,513 households in five provinces (cited by Bredenberg 2003, p.10). Identifying the factors causing students to drop out from school, the study found that financial factors were cited with comparable frequency by both boys and girls (27.4% among boys, and 26.6% among girls). However, work in households was cited more frequently among girls as a reason for dropout (8.1% for boys and 20.7% for girls). A subsequent UNICEF study (Velasco 2001, pp.4, 6) presented similar findings. For example, one government official reflected a widespread view with the remark that girls:

> are expected to help their mothers in housework, child care and the work in the field. Household responsibilities increase as they get older and affect school attendance and performance. They will become discouraged and later drop out from school.

Likewise, illustrating a common view among parents was the remark that:

> When parents are too poor, daughters should stop going to school because they can help in housework and in earning income. The boys can continue their schooling as they are not as capable in housework compared to girls. They cannot do a lot of work.

The 1999 Cambodia Socio-Economic Survey (CSES), which was administered to 6,000 randomly selected households from a stratified sample of 600 randomly selected villages in all 24 provinces and municipalities, provided valuable statistical data on child labour. About 42 per cent of the children aged 14-17 years worked or had a job from which they were temporarily absent during the survey reference week. This included children who worked for wages, profits, dividends or any other kind or payment, or who worked as unpaid family workers (but excluding household chores), for at least one hour during the survey week. The proportion of children aged 5-9 years who worked or had a job was negligible at 2-3 per cent, while the proportion in the 10-13 age group was 9-10 per cent (UNDP 2000, p.28). In the 14-17 age group, about one half of all girls worked, compared with only one third of all boys. Child labour was much more common in rural than in urban areas, the incidence being 29 per cent of girls aged 14-17 in urban areas, but 53 per cent in rural areas. For boys the corresponding ratios were 17 and 39 per cent. In proportion to the population, child labour was greatest in the mountain plateau zone (including Mondulkiri and Ratanakiri Provinces) and lowest in Phnom Penh.

Further statistics were provided by the 2001 Cambodia Child Labour Survey (CCLS), which collected data from 26,000 children aged five to 17 in both urban and rural areas (National Institute of Statistics 2002). Among children aged 6 to 11, 27.6 per cent were reported to be working 14 or more hours per week (Table 21). For children aged 12 to 14 the figure rose to 59.6 per cent, and for children aged 15 to 17 it was 75.7 per cent. Across all age groups, the figures for boys and girls were very similar. Most of the work was unpaid family labour, but some children received paid employment in which average daily earnings in the three groups were 1,594 riels, 2,648 riels and 4,354 riels.

The CCLS also provided information on the match between schooling and work. In the group aged 12 to 14, for example, 3.1 per cent of pupils were neither in school nor working. By contrast, 12.7 per cent were not in school and were undertaking productive and/or domestic work. A further 54.5 per cent were in school but also undertaking productive and/or domestic work; and 29.8 per cent were in school and not undertaking any work. This diversity of situations exposes the complexity: schooling did not necessarily preclude work, and out-of-school children were not necessarily working. Some gender differences were evident, but they were not substantial.

Keng's (2004a) study of two villages in Pursat province provides further empirical case-study data to supplement these observations. Baku and Prinkpus villages are located 17 kilometres from the provincial town and 12 kilometres from the district centre. Their economies are based on subsistence farming supplemented by fishing, growing sugar, and making brooms, mats and roofing thatch. In Baku, during 2003 only 77.3 per cent of primary-school-aged boys and 72.3 per cent of girls attended school; and in Prinkpus respective figures were 85.5 per cent of boys and 58.0 per cent of girls.

Table 21: School and Work Activities of Children, by Gender and Age Group

	----- Both Sexes -----			-------- Boys --------			-------- Girls ------		
	Age 6-11	*Age 12-14*	*Age 15-17*	*Age 6-11*	*Age 12-14*	*Age 15-17*	*Age 6-11*	*Age 12-14*	*Age 15-17*
Schooling									
% enrolled in school	70.3	84.3	52.1	70.3	85.9	61.8	70.3	82.7	41.7
Of those not enrolled, % never enrolled (as opposed to dropout)	98.5	58.0	21.5	99.0	63.1	19.6	98.9	53.6	22.9
Productive Work									
% working >= 14 hours per week	27.6	59.6	75.7	27.7	59.4	74.6	27.4	59.8	77.0
Average hours worked per week if currently working	18.9	24.0	32.4	19.2	24.2	31.1	18.6	23.7	33.9
Type of employment if currently working									
% paid employment	0.7	2.6	9.5	0.8	2.4	7.6	0.5	2.9	11.5
% self-employed/employer	0.9	2.1	5.2	1.2	2.0	4.2	0.6	2.3	6.3
% unpaid family worker	91.5	89.1	79.4	91.2	88.9	82.6	92.0	89.2	75.9
% casual paid	2.7	3.4	4.0	2.8	3.5	4.3	2.7	3.4	3.7
% casual unpaid	4.2	2.8	1.0	4.1	3.3	1.3	4.2	2.3	2.5
Average daily earnings (if paid, in riels)	1,594	2,648	4,354	1,889	3,000	4,149	1,311	2,336	4,516
Domestic Work									
% working >= 14 hours per week	11.0	24.8	36.9	10.2	21.7	30.9	11.7	27.9	43.4
Average hours worked per week if currently working	8.1	10.0	12.1	8.0	9.7	11.1	8.3	10.4	13.1
School and Work Activities (Current)									
% not in school or working	23.3	3.1	4.3	23.5	3.1	4.6	23.0	3.1	4.0
% not in school + prod. & domestic work	2.1	4.1	16.2	1.8	3.1	10.5	2.3	5.0	22.3
% not school + productive work only	3.4	7.2	24.4	3.4	6.7	21.3	3.4	7.6	27.7
% not in school and domestic work only	0.9	1.4	3.1	0.9	1.2	1.9	1.0	1.7	4.4
% in school + productive & domestic work	5.1	13.2	12.6	4.9	12.3	14.1	5.3	14.2	11.0
% in school + productive work only	17.0	35.2	22.6	17.5	37.3	28.8	16.4	33.0	15.9
% in school + domestic work only	2.9	6.1	5.0	2.5	5.2	4.5	3.2	7.0	5.6
% in school and no work	45.4	29.8	11.9	45.3	31.2	14.5	45.4	28.5	9.1

Source: Cambodia Child Labour Survey (2001), cited in World Bank (2004), p.47.

When investigating the determinants of non-enrolment and drop-out, Keng examined the economic circumstances of households as measured by the size of farmland and the number of cattle owned by the families. The size of farmland was positively associated with the likelihood of children remaining in school beyond Grade 4, implying that better endowed households were able to afford to keep their children in school. However, this model did not indicate a significant relationship between the number of cattle owned by the family and the years of children's schooling. Keng pointed out that while on the one hand the children whose families have few or no cattle may have to leave school because they cannot afford the cost, their counterparts in families which own many cattle may have to leave school to look after the cattle. Both in-school and out-of-school children engaged in household chores such as cleaning, fetching water and cooking, and in productive work such as farming, raising pigs and crafting. On average, children spent two to three hours a day on these tasks, and out-of-school children spent only 11 per cent more time on the tasks than in-school children (Keng 2004a, p.8). However, the nature of the work differed. As Keng explained in a different article (2004b, p.10):

> Most girls who minded cattle would have to be absent from school due to the far distance from home and school and the time spent on tasks. After the plowing season is over, cattle are usually taken further away from the village to the unfarmed fields where grass can be found to feed cattle. These girls who had to carry out this task would have to travel with their cattle far away from home and school. Due to the increase in cattle theft, girls had to stay guarding their cattle until late afternoon.

Keng added that 25.0 per cent of the drop-outs' families owned five or more cattle, while only 17.8 per cent of the school-going group did so.

Research in China has reached similar findings. Wang (2001, p.12) used children's main activities after dropping out as an indicator to reflect the influence of opportunity costs on schooling. In the part of Gansu Province which he investigated, relatively few primary-school-aged dropouts engaged in farming or outside work, but the proportion increased significantly for the lower secondary age group. Most dropouts helped their families with agricultural planting, but since this was a seasonal activity the out-of-school children were underemployed. Also, there were few wage-earning employment opportunities in the region, and the interviewed families had little expectation of finding jobs. On this basis, Wang considered the opportunity costs to be low. Nevertheless, the costs can be significant in some families. Interviewees for a follow-up study (Bray et al. 2004) indicated that opportunity costs were not only a matter of planting and paid labour: as in Cambodia, they were also a matter of herding animals. Some children helped their families to gain significant incomes by looking after sheep, and other families earned significant income through trading. A parallel study in Ningxia Province noted that none of the children of the richest family attended school because they all helped their parents with business in the township (Zhou et al. 2003).

Table 22: Over-Age Enrolments, by Level, Location, Gender and Income Group

	Grade 1		% Over-age Enrolment	
	Average Age (Years)	*% Over-age*	*Primary*	*Lower Secondary*
Total	7.6	72.3	40.1	78.3
Urban	7.2	62.2	36.5	73.7
Rural	7.6	74.4	41.9	80.5
Males	7.6	72.3	41.9	82.1
Females	7.6	72.2	38.1	71.7
Poorest	7.7	76.2	41.2	83.5
Quintile 2	8.2	82.5	39.9	87.1
Quintile 3	7.6	71.0	42.4	79.1
Quintile 4	7.3	72.6	41.6	73.1
Richest	6.8	53.4	35.1	72.3

Source: Cambodia Child Labour Survey (2001), cited in World Bank (2004), p.73.

Given that opportunity costs increase with the age of students, the fact that a large proportion of pupils in Cambodian schools are older than the official age is of some importance. Figures from the 2001 Cambodia Child Labour Survey were cited above concerning the age of Grade 1 entrants, and are elaborated on in Table 22. Rural children were older than urban ones right from the start, and thus had higher opportunity costs of schooling. Males and females started at almost the same proportions, but as time proceeded many females dropped out because of the higher opportunity costs that they faced, leaving a lower proportion of over-age pupils still in the system. Among income groups, pupils from the lowest quintiles started at older ages, and thus had higher opportunity costs throughout their school careers. Many of them did survive into lower secondary education; but the table shows the average ages of those who remained in the system rather than those who had been forced to drop out.

Government Funds and Other School-Level Receipts

In addition to household expenditures are various other funds which are received at the school level. The most important of them are resources from the government. In addition are resources from a range of NGOs, and some schools generate their own funds through entrepreneurial and other activities. This section looks first at receipts from government salaries, the PAP, and the Education Quality Improvement Project (EQIP). It then notes resources for capital works, many of which came from the government but others of which came from NGOs and communities; and thirdly it remarks on school-generated incomes.

Salaries, PAP and EQIP Funds

At the national level, statistics are available on overall budgets for education and on PAP disbursements, as portrayed, for example, in Tables 5 and 6. The survey on which this book reports permitted documentation of these matters from the other end, i.e. on what is received at the school level.

Table 23 shows salary receipts at the school level, divided by the official enrolments of the schools to show receipts per pupil. As one might expect, the amounts are greater at lower secondary than at the primary level, reflecting the higher qualifications of lower secondary teachers. However, the figures also show some provincial variations, particularly at the lower secondary level. The statistics must of course be interpreted with some caution. Variations may arise because particular schools are staffed above or below standard norms; and since the figures show receipts per pupil, they do not show clearly the total incomes of teachers because they do not indicate the average class sizes. Nevertheless, the figures are useful for calculating the total balance of resource inputs in the education system. Together with the PAP funds which are disbursed to individual schools, and the government expenditures on overall operation and management of the education system, they can be set alongside the expenditures by households to see the balance of costs in schooling.

Table 23: Average Salary Receipts per Pupil, 2003/04, Riels

	Primary	Lower Secondary
Phnom Penh	42,800	78,800
Takeo	33,200	64,600
Kampot	35,800	101,100
Battambang	47,200	101,700
Banteay Meanchey	36,100	51,800
Svay Rieng	31,000	85,400
Ratanakiri	26,100	95,700
Stung Treng	47,400	83,000
Kandal	38,700	65,400
Kampong Speu	37,500	110,200
Kampong Thom	43,100	114,400
Kampong Cham	62,500	150,800
Average	*39,100*	*86,200*

Table 24, on PAP receipts per pupil, shows more consistency between provinces than Table 23, though also some significant ranges. These figures gloss over the various categories of PAP allocations, and school directors themselves tended to be unclear about the basis on which the allocations were made. Officials in Phnom Penh distinguished between grants (PAP 2.1) and funds for remedial classes (PAP 2.2). Grants were designed for distribution partly on a per school basis and partly on a per capita basis. The official from 2002 onwards (revised from 2000 and 2001)rates were 500,000 riels for each primary school and 1,000,000 riels for each lower secondary school; and 6,000 riels for each primary pupil and 13,600 for each lower secondary pupil. PAP allocations for remedial classes were based on the number of

Grade 1 repeaters at the end of the preceding year. Nevertheless, average per capita PAP receipts are still worth noting because they can then be set alongside average per capita receipts for salaries and average per capita household expenditures.

Table 24: Average PAP Receipts per Pupil, 2003/04 (Riels)

	Primary	Lower Secondary
Phnom Penh	6,096	11,151
Takeo	5,204	9,833
Kampot	3,944	14,478
Battambang	4,886	14,050
Banteay Meanchey	3,672	9,038
Svay Rieng	3,950	8,518
Ratanakiri	3,944	10,949
Stung Treng	6,114	19,907
Kandal	4,596	12,699
Kampong Speu	5,169	11,956
Kampong Thom	6,077	10,883
Kampong Cham	5,863	18,440
Average	*4,962*	*12,197*

These figures on PAP receipts as recorded at the school level can usefully be set alongside figures on PAP disbursements as reported by the authorities in Phnom Penh and recorded in Table 6. That table indicated problems of disbursement of allocations in 2002, with some categories having disbursements below 40 per cent. School directors and teachers were not always clear about the amounts which they could have anticipated, and when funds arrived the directors and teachers were not always certain whether those funds were the allocations for the previous year which were arriving late or the allocations for the current year which were arriving on time.

For present purposes, however, the importance of the figures in Table 24 lies in two domains. First is that these funds did reach the schools. The PAP was particularly designed to replace the charges that schools had previously imposed on households, and so both the existence and the magnitude of the PAP funds need to be noted. Second is the fact that the receipts for lower secondary education were over twice those for primary education. This was appropriate, given that the household costs of lower secondary education were correspondingly higher than those of primary education.

The third element in this category covers funds from EQIP. This project, which operated with assistance from the World Bank, was launched in Takeo Province in 1998/99 with a pilot group of 10 clusters of primary schools (Geeves et al. 2002). In 2000/01 it was expanded to cover all primary schools in Takeo, Kampot and Kandal Provinces, and during the following three years provided cash grants that were invested in priorities determined by the participants as part of their school cluster development plans. The grants were initially 9,700 riels (US$2.56) per pupil per annum though were subsequently reduced to 7,700 riels (Marshall 2004, p.13). Evaluation of the project showed not only that it had had a significant effect through increasing resources at the school level, but also that it had upgraded school management capacities by exposing personnel to experiences in participatory planning.

Capital Works

The 1997/98 study (Bray 1999a) contained appendices which set out on a school-by-school basis the nature of the buildings, the costs of construction, and the sources of funds for construction. These were divided into four categories according to the sources of funds:

- *Government.* Only five out of 77 schools (6.5%) had buildings which had been constructed during the 1990s by the government, and four of the five were in Phnom Penh. Eleven out of 59 schools (18.6%) indicated receipt of some furniture from government sources during recent years.
- *Politicians.* The 1997/98 survey was conducted during a period of intense rivalry between political parties, and the education sector was a major arena for this rivalry. Among the 77 schools, 31 (40.3%) had received school buildings from one or more politicians during the mid-1990s. In 25 of these 31 schools, Hun Sen, then Second Prime Minister, was specifically named. In 10 cases, the whole school had been named or renamed after a politician. In some cases the politicians were reported to have paid for all construction, and also in some in-

stances for furnishings; but in other cases communities provided counterpart resources. Because the politicians did not
usually declare the sources of their funds in an explicit way, it
was difficult to know whether they were drawing on government revenues. It seemed likely that a large part of the finance
came from alternative sources, including donations by business
people who wished to support particular political parties and/or
individuals.

- *NGOs and other external agencies.* During the 1990s, many
  NGOs and external agencies had commenced work in Cambodia. Many of them had included schools in their focus, and had
  provided finance for both capital and recurrent needs. Some of
  these bodies were relatively small, such as World Vision and
  Redd Barna; but others such as UNICEF and the Asian Development Bank were large multilateral organisations. In 43
  (55.8%) of the 77 schools examined, buildings had been constructed by NGOs and/or external aid agencies. In many cases,
  the agencies also provided furniture.

- *Communities.* In many cases, communities had contributed to
  the construction of buildings, particularly in the form of labour
  but also in some cases with materials. For one school in Kampong Cham, each family had been taxed in rice to pay for a
  new building. Other schools recorded donations of cement,
  wood, sand, bricks, furniture and sports materials. Some
  schools had links with Overseas Khmer who had left the country during civil war of the 1970s or at other times and who
  were willing to repatriate resources to help their homeland.

The 2004 survey took a difficult approach to analysis of capital
works. Table 25 shows investments in buildings across a decade (1994-
2003) rather than in a single year, because buildings should be durable
capital investments with long life-spans. It is a rough estimate, because
in some cases assumptions had to be made about the costs of buildings
and because the average per-pupil expenditures were calculated using
the number of pupils in 2003. Nevertheless, the table does provide useful data to set alongside calculations of other per pupil expenditures.

Table 25: Average Annual Building Investments per Pupil, 1994-2003 (Riels)

	Average annual capital expenditure per pupil	
	Primary	Lower Secondary
Phnom Penh	90,118	57,380
Takeo	369,422	269,994
Kampot	223,690	208,710
Battambang	250,942	336,569
Banteay Meanchey	190,711	251,871
Svay Rieng	157,252	219,857
Ratanakiri	231,543	603,291
Stung Treng	61,570	142,222
Kandal	151,973	224,840
Kampong Speu	262,044	317,814
Kampong Thom	317,974	41,137
Kampong Cham	262,928	76,431
Average	*183,051*	*182,790*

The fact that per pupil investments in Phnom Penh are relatively low may be explained by the possibility that many buildings had already been constructed before 1994, but more strongly by the facts that classes were large and that the majority of schools operated double or even triple shifts. In other parts of the country, variations would have arisen from the needs of particular institutions and the availability of donors. Instructively, the figures in Table 25 show a slightly higher per-pupil investment for primary schools than for lower secondary schools.

The government's Education Sector Support Program included investments in buildings alongside other investments. The MoEYS was collaborating with the ADB, the World Bank, NGOs and the private sector, and in 2002/03 envisaged investment of US$5.4 million in rehabilitation of primary school facilities, US$5.0 million in new primary school facilities, and US$2.1 million in new secondary school facilities (MoEYS 2003, p.67). The document appeared to envisage that this construction would be achieved without household inputs.

Enterprises and Other School-Generated Incomes

Schools in Cambodia, as elsewhere, do have some other sources of income. They are not large, but are at least worth noting. Urban schools usually have more opportunities to secure additional incomes than do rural or remote schools. Schools commonly rent food stalls to contractors, and sometimes also rent out bicycle parks. They may also charge users for rent of buildings when the school is not in session. Bak Touk School, in Phnom Penh, was able to earn over 40 million riels per annum through such mechanisms. By contrast, rural schools may earn money from school gardens and in other ways.

Table 26 summarises the data from the survey on incomes per pupil generated through other means. Variations were evident around the country, but in all cases lower secondary schools earned more than primary schools. In most settings, per-pupil school-generated revenues were very small.

Table 26: Other Sources of Income per Pupil, by Province, 2003 (Riels)

	Primary	Lower Secondary
Phnom Penh	3,229	8,811
Takeo	374	532
Kampot	118	223
Battambang	359	991
Banteay Meanchey	361	2,576
Svay Rieng	328	790
Ratanakiri	181	6,131
Stung Treng	1,058	3,413
Kandal	241	916
Kampong Speu	203	5,286
Kampong Thom	361	1,352
Kampong Cham	449	8,282
Average	*1,151*	*3,729*

Balances between Household and Government Financing

The figures presented above can be used for two types of comparison. First, at the primary level estimates of the distribution of sources of funding for primary education in 1997/98 can be compared with those for 2004; and second, the data for primary education in 2004 can be compared with those for lower secondary education.

The 1997/98 study provided a breakdown of expenditures in several categories, including NGOs and politicians. For present purposes, it is adequate simply to present the balance between government and household financing. The two left-hand bar charts in Figure 5 show the balance between government and household financing of primary education in 1997/98 and in 2004;[2] and the two right-hand bar charts compare the balance between primary and lower secondary schooling in 2004. The estimates for government expenditure in 2004 are taken from MoEYS documentation (MoEYS 2004b, p.46). The figures for household costs are taken from Tables 16 and 17, above, weighted to reflect the fact that only about 16 per cent of the population lives in urban areas.

Figure 5: Balances between Household and Government Financing, 1997/98 and 2004, Primary and Lower Secondary Schooling

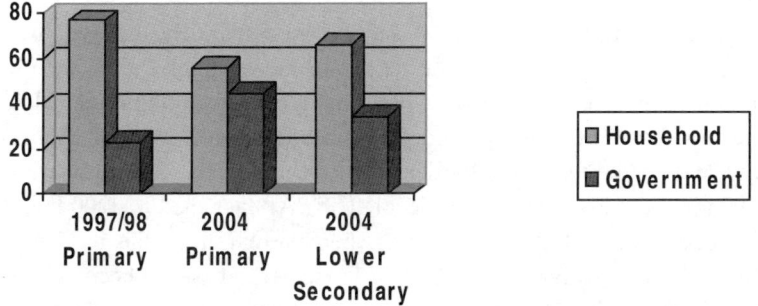

The figures that result from this calculation must be treated with caution because they rest on many assumptions about data accuracy and population distribution, but they are nevertheless instructive. They suggest that in 2004 households were still meeting more of the total costs than the government, but that the gap had considerably narrowed at the primary level. Thus in 2004, out of the combined resources of households and government, households were meeting 55.6 per cent com-

---

2   As noted above, in 1997/98 large amounts of funding were provided by politicians. It was difficult to know how much was contributed from their own resources, and how much from government funds. Figure 5 assumes that half of the funds provided by politicians came from government funds.

pared with 76.9 per cent in 1997/98. In lower secondary schools during 2004 the gap was wider than in primary schools, with households meeting 65.9 per cent; but the gap was not as wide as it had been in primary schools during 1997/98.

Also to be noted is that this study has taken a more complete view of household costs than is sometimes the case. Thus, one official source suggested that in 2004 the MoEYS was meeting 82.1 per cent of the total costs of primary schooling (MoEYS 2004b, p.46). This proportion is very different from that shown in Figure 5, presumably because the MoEYS estimate did not include such a complete listing of household expenditures.

Policy Implications

Patterns identified by the 2004 survey were radically different from those identified in 1997/98. During the 1990s, even after allowance for inputs from donors and others, households were meeting over half of the total costs of primary schooling through a wide array of charges; and in absolute terms the burden of household costs was considerably heavier at the lower secondary level. The PAP launched in 2000 helped to cover many of these costs and thereby to relieve the burden on households. The system of PAP disbursements has not been without problems, but the PAP as a whole has had a strong impact. Reduction of household costs, and the publicity surrounding that reduction, was among the major factors leading to increased enrolments at both primary and lower secondary levels in 2000 and subsequent years.

The above data show, however, that many household costs remain. The question then becomes whether further action is needed by the government, and if so of what sort. The answers require consideration of a number of variables.

Philosophies on Cost-Sharing

A necessary starting point concerns basic philosophies on cost-sharing. As indicated above, many international pronouncements and various individual analysts assert the importance of fee-free basic education for all. However, other policy-makers and practitioners are less insistent on this goal. They argue that nobody should be prevented from attending school by the existence of charges, but that some charges might be desirable in order to encourage recipients of services to value those services more highly than they otherwise would do. They add that excessive government provision leads to a hand-out mentality. For example, Swartland and Taylor (1988, p.151) analysed the effects of increased government funding of community junior secondary schools in Botswana:

> Increased government support too easily turns into conformity and control. It also heightens expectations of what government can and should do and reinforces a dependent mentality rather than one of self-reliance. Having got subsidies, teachers, and buildings from the government, the schools are now asking for film projectors, security fences, "official-free" stamps, school vehicles, and graders to level their sports fields.

Similarly, in Malawi a Free Primary Education (FPE) scheme launched by the government in 1994 undermined community participation. As reported by Rose (2003, p.56):

> In many cases, communities felt that FPE means that it is now the responsibility of the government to provide facilities so that, at some schools, communities were reluctant to be involved in construction and maintenance where they were previously willing to contribute.... Although community participation is commonly believed to play an important role in fostering democracy, there is evidence that democracy, as it is perceived in Malawi particularly in the context of FPE, is having a detrimental effect on community participation in primary schooling.

On a related tack with reference to Uganda, Suzuki (2002a, p.168) noted that fee-free education can contribute to dismissive attitudes among teachers. One parent in her survey explained that:

> There is this mentality some teachers in this school have, that a child may bring a book to a teacher [for marking] to whom the teacher says 'You go away! After all you are studying for free'.

> This thing hurts us parents. Maybe lack of parents bringing those
> things [contribution for schools and teachers] is what causes this
> teacher's attitude.

Of course even if the parents were paying something, the teachers might
still claim that the parents were not paying enough; but Suzuki's research shows a negative side of the fee-free education scheme launched
in Uganda in 1997 that has in other settings attracted so much approval
(see e.g. World Bank 2001, p.33; Tomasevski 2003, pp.136-139).

In this connection, in Cambodia the dominance of government
financing which emerged with the reforms of 2000 onwards may have
undermined some desirable facets of earlier patterns. The 1997/98 study
(Bray 1999a) noted the strong community spirit in many schools including the links between schools and pagodas. Variations were evident
according to local circumstances and to the leadership of specific individuals and groups, but instances in which monks and others in the
communities provided financial support to schools were quite common.
With the advent of the PAP, such relationships diminished. The National Education for All Commission (2003, p.25) set a target "to reduce
the parental/community contributions for basic education costs from 22
per cent [in 2002] to 0 per cent by 2015". This zero target should perhaps be reconsidered. While the authorities certainly should do their
best to remove barriers to schooling, some parents and communities are
both able and willing to share the costs of schooling, and the system
benefits when they do so. Among the benefits is the interest that parents
and communities have in schools to which they contribute, and in promoting accountability. In many countries, schools have become exces-
sively separated from the main fabric of society. Parents and communities have a hand-out mentality in which they expect governments to
provide, and merely criticise when operations are less than perfect.

Another reason for welcoming household contributions from those
who are able and willing to pay is that such contributions enlarge the
overall resource base for education. This permits improvements in quality as well as quantity, and can benefit poor groups as well as rich ones.
Government resources may be released for better targeting of the poor,
e.g. through scholarships and construction of schools closer to the
homes of disadvantaged groups. Cambodia currently receives substan-

tial donor resources, but this pattern is not sustainable for the long term. The most appropriate long-term source of revenue for the government will be taxation. The system of taxation has been substantially improved, but for some time it is likely to remain unable to generate all the resources that the government will need for social services and roles. Within the education sector are needs for improved quality at all levels, and for expansion of secondary and tertiary education; and to this must be added the demands of social, economic and other sectors. Thus the government resource base will remain constrained, and inputs from all sides will continue to be needed.

One problem of community and household resourcing, it must be recognised, is that it tends to maintain and exacerbate inequalities because rich communities and households are more easily able to provide resources than are poor ones (Bray 1996b, 2003b; Caillods & Lewin 2001). In some countries, especially ones dominated by Communist governments, this has in the past been a reason for centralising provision in the state and for prohibiting non-state contributions to education systems. However, many policy analysts now advocate decentralisation of provision, and many societies tolerate greater diversity than they did previously (see e.g. McGinn & Welsh 1999; Mok 2003). Policy-makers in Cambodia have committed themselves to aspects of decentralisation (MoEYS 2002a, 2004b; Turner 2002), and centralised prohibition of any sort of community and household financing of schools does not seem easily compatible with this direction.

Scholarships

If some household costs remain, the question becomes how the poorest groups can be protected. Scholarships are among the most obvious answers. Scholarships may aim only to meet some or all direct costs of schooling, or they may aim also to cover some or all opportunity costs. If desired, scholarships can be targeted not only on the poor but also on girls and minority groups.

In Cambodia, no government-sponsored scholarships are available at the primary level, but at the lower secondary level various scholarship schemes have been launched. One of them is part of the Priority

Action Program, known as PAP 12 (see Table 6), and is coordinated with various donor-funded schemes to form a nationwide programme. In 2003/04, each PAP 12 scholarship had a value of 180,000 riels which was disbursed in instalments of 80,000 riels, 60,000 riels and 40,000 riels. The front-end loading was appropriate because many of the direct costs of schooling are incurred particularly heavily at the beginning of each school year. The government subsequently decided to increase the front-end loading to a ratio of 60: 20: 20, i.e. 108,000 riels in the first instalment and 36,000 in the two subsequent instalments. The authorities planned that by 2010 the scheme would cover 1,140 schools at a cost of 16.7 billion riels (MoEYS 2003, p.124). In 2003/04, PAP 12 provided 30 scholarships to each of 215 lower secondary schools in 16 provinces. This amounted to 6,450 scholarships, of which 60 per cent were designated for girls and 40 per cent for boys.

The second major group of scholarships was financed by the Japan Fund for Poverty Reduction (JFPR) in conjunction with the ADB, and in 2003/04 targeted 93 lower secondary schools in 21 provinces. In 75 of these schools scholarships were only available for girls, while in the remaining 18 schools 60 per cent of scholarships were for girls and 40 per cent were for boys. The programme provided 75 scholarships to each school: 45 in Grade 7 and 30 in Grade 8.

The third source of funds was Belgian Technical Cooperation, which targeted 80 schools in three provinces, namely Kampong Cham, Siem Reap and Otdar Meanchey. It initially provided 30 scholarships per school for Grade 7, with 60 per cent of the scholarships being allocated to girls and 40 per cent to boys. Subsequently, scholarships were allocated on a per commune basis with priority being given to the poorer communes.

The scholarship schemes have a short history and thus cannot yet be fully evaluated. Nevertheless, some general observations can be made. First is that the amounts of the scholarships barely cover the direct costs of lower secondary schooling in rural areas, and are unable to cover the direct costs in either urban or remote areas. Further, even if they do cover the direct costs, they cannot cover the opportunity costs of schooling.

The survey for this study found that some students had received scholarships but had nevertheless dropped out of school. The survey did not find cases in which students had dropped out because they were still unable to meet all direct costs. Rather, the opportunity costs seemed to be more important. The three main reasons for leaving school were:

- *Finding a good job:* Some pupils were already 16 or 17 years old when they commenced lower secondary school. If jobs were available, families often preferred to take those jobs than to stay in the education system. Common types of work undertaken included domestic service in Phnom Penh, factory employment, and work in restaurants in Phnom Penh or tourist areas.

- *Change of residence:* Poor families must seek economic opportunities, and many resettle in new economic areas such as Phnom Penh, Siem Reap and Poipet. When children migrate, they have to leave the schools in which they were originally studying. In some cases, the families try to transfer the children to new schools, but this is often difficult. Since at the same time the families need help with labour, they commonly decide to withdraw their children from school.

- *Marriage:* Girls commonly marry early in Cambodia. When they get married, they have to leave school.

Thus two of these three major reasons concern opportunity costs, while the third is cultural.

However, these observations do not necessarily suggest that the scholarships should be increased to cover opportunity costs. First, it is more difficult to set an appropriate standard level, since the opportunity costs for each family would differ. Second, if the amounts of individual scholarships were raised, then fewer individuals would be able to receive scholarships. And third, although eventually the government may wish to target groups who would not go to school without their opportunity costs being covered, in the present situation so many children do not go to lower secondary school that the scholarships can be used more effectively to target those who are relatively easy to encourage.

At the same time, the decisions to target particular geographic areas and to focus on girls have strong justifications. Poor households of course exist in middle-income and even prosperous areas, but since they are concentrated in poor areas they are easier to reach within limited budgets. Similarly boys as well as girls encounter financial obstacles; but girls are clearly more vulnerable than boys, and are currently under-represented in the education system.

On a different tack, during the focus group discussions respondents noted problems of cash flow for recurrent expenses such as food and snacks. These people suggested that scholarship disbursements could be made every month rather than three times a year. However, this would increase administrative costs, and the existing pattern of disbursements three times a year may provide the optimum balance from an administrative perspective.

Nevertheless, some other administrative dimensions deserve stress. As Bredenberg (2003, pp.13-14) pointed out, it is essential for payments to be punctual:

> Poor scholarship candidates will likely drop out early in the school year if funds are not received promptly; that is, they will not wait 6 months or more for a payment, especially one that only covers 50% of total costs.

He added that the belief by some that the promise of such payments, even if tardy, would help motivate families to keep their children in school was generally thought to be highly unrealistic by field level observers.

Finally, the above discussion focuses on scholarships for lower secondary schooling. As noted, no government scholarships are available for primary schooling, though a few have been provided by NGOs (MoEYS & KAPE 2001, p.15). The government has done much to remove the direct costs of schooling, but for the poorest of the poor a case can be made for scholarships to cover at least some opportunity costs. Models elsewhere show that such inputs do not necessarily have to be in cash. In Bangladesh, for example, children have been given wheat and rice (World Bank 2000; Arends-Kuenning & Amin 2004). However, it must be recognised that scholarship schemes can be major budgetary commitments which bring administrative complexities, and the Cambodian government should not embark on such a scheme without careful consideration.

Private Tutoring

The government has long been ambivalent about private tutoring, and in the mid-1990s even endeavoured to prohibit the practice. However, prohibition could not be enforced; and for the time being the authorities seem to view tutoring as an endemic practice that is largely beyond their control.

Any policy on tutoring has to be linked to teachers' salaries. When salaries are so low that teachers cannot feed their families on their official earnings, the teachers are forced to find ways to supplement their incomes. Private tutoring is more widespread in urban than rural and remote areas not only because urban societies are more competitive and therefore demand for tutoring is greater, but also because living costs are higher and teachers are under more pressure to secure supplementary incomes and therefore wish to supply tutoring. Another factor is that average incomes are higher and therefore that many urban households are able to pay more easily than their rural and remote counterparts. Thus, teachers in rural and remote areas who consider encouraging or demanding pupils to take private tutoring are more likely to abandon the idea simply because incomes are lower and their pupils cannot so easily pay.

Private tutoring is increasingly coming into focus worldwide as an issue with many facets. Even in prosperous societies such as Hong Kong, Singapore, South Korea and Taiwan, a great deal of tutoring is undertaken, with consequent implications for household budgets. As in Cambodia, policy makers in these societies are ambivalent about the phenomenon. On the one hand, they respect the right of rich households to invest in extra education for their children in order to assist those children in the competitive society; but on the other hand they are mindful of the impact on social stratification, and note that poor families may find themselves forced to invest in tutoring simply to allow their children to remain in the educational race. However, one major difference between these societies and Cambodia is that teachers are prohibited from tutoring the children for whom those teachers already have responsibility in mainstream classes. This avoids the sorts of blackmail circumstances that can and do arise in Cambodia, in which teachers deliberately cover only part of syllabuses during mainstream classes in order to promote demand for their after-school private lessons. Prohibition along these lines would seem to be an important move for the Cambodian authorities to consider; but it can only be contemplated if teachers are given an adequate salary in the first place, and are not forced to provide tutoring simply to secure adequate incomes to feed their families.

Because of its focus, the 1997/98 book only highlighted the extent and nature of tutoring at primary level (Bray 1999a, pp.57-60). The addition of lower secondary schooling in this study brings a further dimension. At primary level, most tutoring covers the syllabus as a whole; but tutors at the secondary level, like classroom teachers, are more likely to specialise in particular subjects. As indicated above, the survey found that the four most popular subjects were mathematics, physics, chemistry and Khmer literature, plus English in urban areas. This has implications for the attractiveness of certain subjects to candidates entering the teaching profession. The corollary of some subjects being popular, and thus able to provide extra incomes through supplementary classes, is that other subjects are relatively unpopular and unable to generate such incomes. However, from the perspective of national development it is arguable that subjects such as history, geography, biology and physical education are also important. It is regrettable if market forces undermine the quality and quantity of instruction in those subjects.

The Priority Action Programme

In general, the respondents in this research expressed considerable satisfaction with the PAP. As might be expected, they did not all understand the details of its design and operation; but they observed many dimensions in which it had had a very positive impact.

However, school directors and teachers raised a number of concerns which deserve reporting. On matters of implementation, they highlighted three major issues:

- *Payment delays:* Personnel in both primary and secondary schools complained about delays in the payment of PAP funds. Faced by such delays and the need to survive, some schools had started again to collect contributions from parents. The MoEYS was itself aware of this matter, recognising in 2003 for example that "PAP disbursement is unreliable and unpredictable which undermines the potential for de-centralisation and quality improvement", and that "the complicated allocation trail is not transparent enough" (MoEYS 2003, p.47). It is worth emphasising, however, that much good work can be wasted if the flow of funds does not proceed in a smooth and timely manner to the schools.

- *Limited categories of PAP funds:* The schools outlined the limitations of PAP funding categories, which were fixed by the regulations. Respondents felt that they needed more flexibility to meet the needs of specific circumstances. For example, some institutions are more in need of repairs and maintenance than others; and under the regulations schools are unable e.g. to make seasonal one-off investments in sports equipment.

- *Lack of accounting skills:* Most schools pointed out that the MoEYS financial procedures were too complicated. Bookkeepers in many schools felt that their previous training was not sufficient and needed upgrading.

The PAP has also impacted negatively on teachers' incomes, especially in rural areas. As indicated, before the creation of the PAP teachers were able to supplement their incomes by selling monthly test papers and other learning materials. This is no longer permitted; and the PAP funds which are designed to replace such household costs go to the schools rather than the teachers. The remote teachers experience less of a problem in this respect since their pupils were in general too poor to pay the various supplementary charges, and the PAP has made the schools in the remote areas better off than they were before. The urban teachers are also less worried about the loss of income from the prohibition since they can still undertake supplementary tutoring. Thus, the greatest loss of income is experienced by the rural teachers.

Conclusions

This book has pointed out that Cambodia has many achievements in the education sector which deserve celebration. The first part in this concluding section highlights some of these achievements. At the same time, of course, Cambodia faces many ongoing challenges, some of which are considered in the second part. The third part presents further comments on the nature of household decision-making; and the final part remarks on the ongoing search for appropriate balances both in Cambodia and elsewhere.

Achievements to be Celebrated

The reconstruction of Cambodia's education system since the end of the Pol Pot era, and particularly since the early 1990s, is a remarkable story for which the Cambodian government and people are to be admired. The government has delivered on promises to reduce expenditures on the military and to increase expenditures on education, and proportions of the government budget and of GDP allocated to education have again reached proportions comparable to those of the 1960s. Cambodia has been assisted in these tasks by considerable aid from bilateral and multilateral sources.

Within this remarkable picture, the expansion of primary and lower secondary enrolments has been especially noteworthy. This has partly been achieved through supply-side initiatives including construction of schools and location of facilities nearer to children's homes. It has also been achieved through demand-side initiatives in which the government has adjusted the balance of costs. The 1997/98 study showed a huge proportional burden on households, even within the public system of education. The shift of that burden achieved by the reforms devised in 2000 was a major stimulus to increased enrolments. At the primary level, moreover, the greatest increases were in poor households (Figure 6).

Figure 6: Primary School New Intakes by Poverty Quintile, 1999-2001

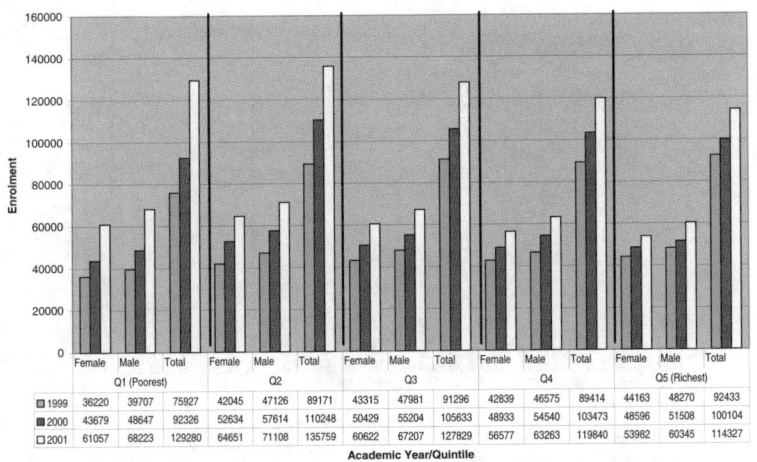

	Q1 (Poorest)			Q2			Q3			Q4			Q5 (Richest)		
	Female	Male	Total	Female	Male	Total	Female	Male	Total	Female	Male	Total	Female	Male	Total
1999	36220	39707	75927	42045	47126	89171	43315	47981	91296	42839	46575	89414	44163	48270	92433
2000	43679	48647	92326	52634	57614	110248	50429	55204	105633	48933	54540	103473	48596	51508	100104
2001	61057	68223	129280	64651	71108	135759	60622	67207	127829	56577	63263	119840	53982	60345	114327

Academic Year/Quintile

Source: MoEYS (2002b), p.8.

In contrast to the primary sector, the greatest enrolment increases in lower secondary schooling were in the higher-income groups (Figure 7). This was partly because the increases were coming from a lower base, and in the first instance the opportunities were grasped by households in higher-income groups. Yet although the initiatives in lower secondary schooling were not as pro-poor as in primary schooling, some poor households benefited. Also, the scholarship schemes launched in 2003 endeavoured to increase the proportion of the poor. Moreover, the increased enrolment of pupils from higher-income groups was still much to be welcomed in the march towards universal basic education.

Concerning gender proportions, Figures 7 and 8 show that in both primary and lower secondary education, boys outnumbered girls in new intakes in every income quintile and in every year. Yet while policy makers were rightly anxious to close the gender gap and thus were concerned about this pattern, boys are important as well as girls. Thus the overall increase in enrolment rates of both genders was to be celebrated.

Figure 7: Lower Secondary School New Intakes by Poverty Quintile, 1999-2001

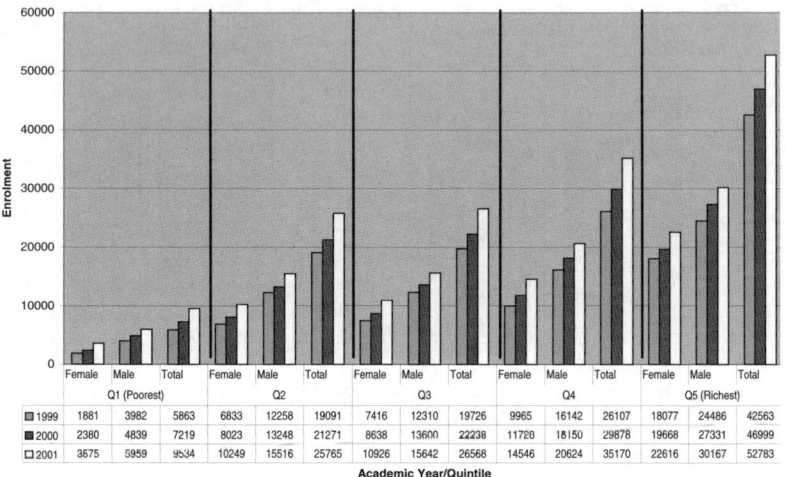

	Q1 (Poorest)			Q2			Q3			Q4			Q5 (Richest)		
	Female	Male	Total	Female	Male	Total	Female	Male	Total	Female	Male	Total	Female	Male	Total
1999	1881	3982	5863	6833	12258	19091	7416	12310	19726	9965	16142	26107	18077	24486	42563
2000	2380	4839	7219	8023	13248	21271	8638	13600	22238	11720	18150	29878	19668	27331	46999
2001	3575	5959	9534	10249	15516	25765	10926	15642	26568	14546	20624	35170	22616	30167	52783

Academic Year/Quintile

Source: MoEYS (2002b), p.13.

Among the instructive features of the enrolment growth was the extent to which demand increased even though the registration and other charges that were removed were not the largest components of the costs of schooling. Other costs, especially uniforms, pocket money, transport and supplementary tutoring, were much more significant. This pattern of responsiveness to changes in registration charges was in line with experiences elsewhere which indicated that fees form a psychological as well as practical barrier. In Peru, for example, Ilon and Moock (1991, p.441) found that parents' decisions were very sensitive to the level of school fees and much less sensitive to ancillary costs such as books and uniforms. Fair (1998, p.207) found a similar pattern in Namibia; and Kadzamira and Rose (2003, p.506) reported comparable findings in Malawi.

A further probable factor in the surge of enrolments was the general publicity at both national and local levels about the removal of charges. At the local level, village leaders disseminated information to households about the new policy and encouraged parents to enrol their children. Such publicity again has parallels elsewhere. As noted above,

Malawi launched a fee-free primary education scheme in 1994, and was followed by Uganda in 1997. Other examples include Nigeria, which launched such a scheme in 1976 and again in 1996; Ghana, which made similar moves in 1961 and 1996; Tanzania, which did likewise in 1977 and 2001; and Kenya, which did so in 1963, 1978 and 2003. In these and other cases, the publicity surrounding the initiatives was an important component in the increased enrolments that resulted.

Challenges Ahead

The experience of other countries which have achieved surges of enrolments through abolition of fees has been that recruitment of children to schools is only the first challenge. The second challenge is to keep the children there for a reasonable duration, i.e. to prevent early dropout. Associated challenges concern provision of facilities, recruitment of teachers, and management of large classes. At the household level, euphoria about the opportunity to enter schools free of charge has often been followed by disillusion about the quality of education in those schools (see e.g. Buckland 2000; Obasi 2000; Rose 2003). The Cambodian authorities are of course aware of these challenges, and are rightly addressing qualitative issues as well as quantitative ones; but the journey is be tough and demanding.

Another common international pattern has been that despite official policies of fee-free education, schools have found themselves starved of resources and have therefore needed to secure non-government incomes simply in order to operate at the most basic level. The result is a duplicitous situation in which schooling is officially free of charge but in which a multitude of 'levies' and 'contributions' are demanded (see e.g. Tilak 1995; Francis et al. 1998; Hannum 2003; Mukudi 2004). At the time of this research, Cambodia seemed largely to be avoiding that pattern. However, the warning signs existed, especially in schools which had not received promised PAP payments in a timely manner. This situation stresses the importance of the government and aid agencies ensuring not only that they make the promised budgetary allocations but also that the funds get through to the schools on time.

Within this framework, a major issue concerns teachers' salaries. As noted above, official salaries are so low that on their own they are inadequate to maintain teachers and their families at levels above the poverty line. Given this situation, it is remarkable that so many teachers have remained in the profession and that the education system has remained intact and operational. The main reason why most teachers have stayed in the system is that they do not have alternatives that are sufficiently attractive and reliable. As Cambodia's economy develops, the number of opportunities will increase. In this respect Cambodia is likely to find itself in a situation experienced elsewhere – that in some respects economic development, in the short run, undermines rather than supports the education system.

In the longer run, however, economic development should be good for the education system. This will particularly be the case if the government has an adequate system of taxation. Very few documents in the education sector, either in Cambodia or internationally, have given sufficient attention to this matter. External aid is of course valuable, but neither should nor can be considered a reliable component for the long term (Burgess 1997, p.309). As noted above, major improvements were made in Cambodia's taxation system during the late 1990s and subsequently, but the ratios of taxation to GDP were still among the lowest in the world. This matter should not be left to the Ministry of Finance and to macro-economists: it should also be a major concern of the MoEYS and of educators. The education sector needs to highlight the importance of improved taxation revenues, and to maintain pressure to secure substantial proportions of those revenues. Once obtained, a major use of the revenues should be improvement of teachers' salaries. Of course that will not solve everything; but at least teachers will not need to undertake private tutoring and seek other ways to raise incomes simply because they have to survive.

This study has also shown that household costs increase markedly when a child makes a transition from primary to lower secondary school. Government efforts have contained many of these costs, but even some of the charges imposed by schools are likely to be ongoing. In this connection, it is useful to note the observation in the report by the MoEYS and KAPE (2001, p.17) that, compared with primary schools:

Secondary schools appear to have much less financial accountability to local communities and tend to be operated like small corporations with a profusion of arbitrarily set fees. This is possibly due to their large catchment areas, making them remote from communities, and the fact that they are managed directly by the Provincial Offices of Education (as opposed to the district offices) which tend to be far away from unhappy community members.

Again, issues of accountability and management come to the fore in this observation.

Household Decision-Making

The initial paragraphs of this book noted that when households are considering whether or not to send their children to school, they make informal assessments of whether the costs of doing so will outweigh the benefits. This is not the only factor, and indeed in some settings it may not even be the most important. Other factors include the nature of the curriculum, the anticipated impact of the school on children's values, the attitudes of neighbours and other influential people, and cultural dimensions such as the usual age of marriage. Yet alongside and sometimes in conjunction with these other factors, informal cost-benefit analyses are certainly important. Especially for the poorest families, the estimation of balances requires consideration not only of the direct costs of schooling but also of the opportunity costs. The direct and indirect household costs reinforce each other to produce a critical barrier for the poor in upper primary and lower secondary schooling.

In making these observations, it is appropriate to ask what is meant by a household and who really makes what decisions. This book has left the definition of households vague, but it recognises that decisions may not be taken by whole households as single entities. Mothers, fathers, uncles, aunts, siblings and others play different roles at different times and perhaps for children of different genders. Moreover, the decision-makers for young children may be different from the decision-makers for older children. Keng (2004a, p.9) pointed out that older children are likely to make their own decisions, and then either to inform or persuade the other household members.

A further qualifying remark must be made about the notion of cost-benefit analyses. While economists may be able to generate precise numerical estimates (see e.g. McMahon 2002; OECD & UNESCO 2003; Psacharopoulos & Patrinos 2004), rare indeed are the households that embark on mathematical assessments. At most, the household assessments are informal and impressionistic. Further, the poorest households may not even do that: they may be so occupied with the short-term demands of subsistence that the notion of long-term benefits is over the horizon. Bredenberg's (2003, p.22) study of demand for education recorded interviewers' impressions of "the grim struggle for survival" that faced many respondents. Most members of focus group discussions, he indicated, seemed profoundly unable to think of life in the long term. Rather, "children and parents tended to think about the obstacles to education in very immediate terms: not enough money this week, planting starts next month, or mother needs me to watch the children tomorrow".

This leads to a question about appropriate roles for the state. One argument for compulsory schooling is that it is good for the society as a whole, from both a social and an economic perspective. Such a view can be used to support state intervention, on the grounds that macroeconomists are able to take long-term views and to see the benefits that can accrue from investment in education even if individual households are not able to take such long-term views (see e.g. World Bank 2003).

While such arguments may have general validity, however, it is desirable to secure convergence between the perspectives of the state and of the households. One major question for households, in Cambodia and elsewhere (see e.g. Fair 1998; Rose & Al-Samarrai 2001; Okuma-Nystrom 2003; Keng 2004a), concerns the nature of the labour market. As education levels rise, so do the entry points to certain occupations. Households may identify 'all or none' situations in which they consider it only worth investing in education if their children can be expected to go beyond the threshold needed to secure the types of remunerative employment that can be expected to give appropriate returns on investment. In many countries, such factors are a major reason why enrolment rates have remained stagnant. Households which do not expect their children to seek some form of cash-earning employment are particularly reluctant to invest in education beyond the primary stage. Bredenberg

(2003, p.28) noted this factor in his study of demand for schooling in Cambodia. Especially in remote areas, he reported:

> both parents and student focus groups noted that a student who finishes secondary school had nothing else to do but to be a farmer if they decided to stay in the local area. There was, therefore, little difference in terms of economic standing between a child who had dropped out early in their schooling and one who had studied to a terminal grade level. Thus, the expenditures of time and financial resources on secondary education could only be a good investment for those who had the means and opportunity to migrate elsewhere; otherwise, such investments rarely seemed to pay off.

In turn, such statements highlight the extent to which education is part of the broader fabric of development, but can contribute to major social disruption through internal migration.

Within this picture, a major element concerns gender (Bredenberg 2003, p.33). In general, both direct and opportunity costs are lowest for small children and increase as the children get older. At the initial stages, costs are more or less equal for both boys and girls, but at later stages opportunity costs are likely to be greater for girls. When age, cultural and other factors are added to the equation, the chances of girls continuing their education to higher grades are progressively diminished.

Finally, it is worth stressing that the costs of schooling for children in remote areas are likely to be much higher than in rural areas. If at the same time the benefits are likely to be lower, remote households have a double reason for not sending their children to school. Over time, this combination of factors is likely to increase geographic and social disparities around the country, and it again points to an important role for the state in promoting equity.

Finding Appropriate Balances

The approach of the Cambodian government and its aid partners, as recounted in this book, has been to grapple with the constraints of development and to move towards the goal of Universal Basic

Education. Major progress has been achieved through both supply-side interventions, such as construction of schools, and demand-side interventions which have sought to encourage households to enrol their children in the schools. A major component in the demand-side interventions has been adjustment of the weights in the balance between costs and benefits. As schooling has become more widespread, the amounts of schooling which must be obtained to secure jobs of particular types has increased. For households, this means a reduction over time of the benefits that they can anticipate from investment in schooling of specific durations. If at the same time the costs are high, the chances of households sending children to school are markedly diminished. Noting that during the 1990s households were bearing very heavy costs, the government has sought to reduce that burden by itself covering an increasing proportion of total costs. Such adjustments to the balance are especially necessary for the poorest households, who under other circumstances would probably not send their children to school.

However, a question remains whether it is appropriate for the government to meet all costs of schooling for all households and at all levels of education. As noted at the beginning of this book, at the post-secondary level the dominant view worldwide is that fees are desirable even in public institutions of education. This is partly because higher income groups tend to be disproportionately represented in post-secondary education, and public subsidies at that level therefore benefit the higher-income groups more than the lower-income ones. To ensure that poor households do nevertheless have access, grants and loans are provided.

One argument for not following such an approach at lower levels of education is administrative – that the costs of operating systems of grants and loans for levels of education which serve more than a minority of students are so great that it is preferable to save the administrative costs and simply provide education free of charge. Another argument is that government resources which are allocated to lower levels of education systems are more likely to be pro-poor than allocations to higher levels, because poor families are more strongly represented at lower levels of education systems since their children have not yet dropped out.

Nevertheless, even at the level of basic education the assertion that fee-free education is necessary to minimise the burden on the poorest households does not necessarily mean that fee-free education is necessary for all households. Indeed, rather to the contrary, it can be argued that medium-income and rich households should at least be permitted – and possibly encouraged and even required – to contribute to the costs of education. This is for several reasons, the first of which concerns government resource base. Countries which have vibrant economies, strong infrastructures for collecting taxes, and a willingness in the general population to pay high taxes, can certainly support not only fee-free basic education but even fee-free higher education. This is the case for example in Denmark and some other countries of Western Europe. However, Cambodia does not have a vibrant economy, does not have a strong infrastructure for collecting taxes, and does not have a general willingness in the general population to pay high taxes. Cambodia therefore faces a challenge to provide universal basic education of even minimum quality.

That observation brings in the second element, namely the qualitative dimension. Many low-income countries have found that fee-free education permits children from poor households to come to school, but then threatens the quality of education once they get there. Surveys have found that many parents are willing to contribute to quality provided that their own children benefit; and national development certainly requires quality in basic education that considerably raises the standards of much that is offered in resource-constrained settings.

Recognising such factors, when the governments of Tanzania and Zambia launched their free-education schemes in 2001 and 2002 respectively, they were careful to state that no child should be excluded because of cost but that Parent-Teacher Associations (PTAs) and school committees were still permitted to demand levies from those who were able and willing to pay (UNESCO 2003, p.221). In Uganda, Suzuki (2002b, p.250) found that despite the government ban on mandatory monetary contributions, many schools collected money through the PTAs. Most of the parents that Suzuki interviewed saw such contributions as "fair" and "necessary", though some parents did not pay either because of economic constraints or because of the perceived lack of accountability by the school.

Along similar lines, the Cambodian authorities would be wise to avoid 'one-size-fits-all' policies, and to seek different balances for different populations. The priority would be to alleviate the burden on the poor by minimising direct costs and perhaps also making subsidies to cover opportunity costs. Yet this does not necessarily mean that the middle-income and rich households should be prohibited from contributing to the costs. Indeed such payments may be desirable not only to balance the accountants' books but also to promote accountability between the schools and their communities. For this reason, the target by the National Education for All Commission (2003, p.25) to reduce the parental and community contributions for basic education to zero should perhaps be reconsidered.

International experience shows that the search for appropriate balances is never-ending because adjustments are constantly needed to fit new circumstances and goals. Also, throughout the world policy makers and practitioners have to grapple with gaps between policies and implementation. This book has shown that the Cambodian government and people have grappled with their own circumstances, and have achieved much that deserves applause. As such, the contents of this book may provide lessons and encouragement to other governments and peoples, as well as within Cambodia itself.

References

Annigeri, V.B. (1998): 'Primary Education: How the Panchayats are Doing?', in Aggarwal, Yash & Premi, Kusum K. (eds.), *Reforming School Education: Issues in Policy Planning and Implementation*. New Delhi: Vikas, pp.40-48.

Arends-Kuenning, Mary & Amin, Sajeda (2004): 'School Incentive Programs and Children's Activities: The Case of Bangladesh'. *Comparative Education Review*, Vol.48, No.3, pp.295-317.

Asian Development Bank (1996): *Cambodia: Education Sector Strategy Study*. Manila: Asian Development Bank.

Ayres, David (2001): Review of Bray, Mark (1999) *The Private Costs of Public Schooling: Household and Community Financing of Primary Education in Cambodia*, in *Education and Society*, Vol.19, No.1, pp.93-95.

Ayres, David (2003): *Anatomy of a Crisis: Education, Development, and the State in Cambodia, 1953-1998*. Chiang Mai: Silkworm Books.

Boyle, S., Brock, A., Mace, J. & Sibbons, M. (2002): *Reaching the Poor: The 'Costs' of Sending Children to School – A Six Country Comparative Study*. London: Department for International Development.

Bray, Mark (1996a): *Counting the Full Cost: Household and Community Financing of Education in East Asia*. Washington DC: The World Bank in collaboration with UNICEF.

Bray, Mark (1996b): *Decentralization of Education: Community Financing*. Washington DC: The World Bank.

Bray, Mark (1999a): *The Private Costs of Public Schooling: Household and Community Financing of Primary Education in Cambodia*. Paris: UNESCO International Institute for Educational Planning [also published in Phnom Penh by UNICEF, 1998, with short version in both English and Khmer]

Bray, Mark (1999b): *The Shadow Education System: Private Tutoring and its Implications for Planners*. Fundamentals of Educational Planning 61, Paris: UNESCO International Institute for Educational Planning.

Bray, Mark (2003a): *Adverse Effects of Private Supplementary Tutoring: Dimensions, Implications and Government Responses*. Paris: UNESCO International Institute for Educational Planning.

Bray, Mark (2003b): 'Community Initiatives in Education: Goals, Dimensions, and Linkages with Governments'. *Compare: A Journal of Comparative Education*, Vol.33, No.1, pp.31-45.

Bray, Mark (2004): *The Costs and Financing of Education: Trends and Policy Implications*. Series: 'Education in Developing Asia'. Hong Kong: Comparative Education Research Centre, The University of Hong Kong, and Manila: Asian Development Bank.

Bray, Mark, Ding, X. & Huang, P. (2004): *Reducing the Burden on the Poor: Household Costs of Basic Education in Gansu, China*. Hong Kong: Comparative Education Research Centre, The University of Hong Kong in association with the Gansu Basic Education Project.

Bray, Mark with Lillis, Kevin (eds.) (1988): *Community Financing of Education: Issues and Policy Implications in Less Developed Countries*. Oxford: Pergamon Press.

Bredenberg, Kurt (2003): 'Cambodia Secondary Education Study: Educational Demand in the Basic Education Sector and Strategies for Enhancement'. Phnom Penh: Kampuchean Action for Primary Education.

Brock, Andy (2001): Review of Bray, Mark (1999) *The Private Costs of Public Schooling: Household and Community Financing of Primary Education in Cambodia*, in *Comparative Education*, Vol.37, No.2, pp.249-250.

Buckland, Peter (2000): *Making Quality Basic Education Affordable: What have we Learned?*. New York: UNICEF.

Burgess, Robin S.L. (1997): 'Fiscal Reform and the Extension of Basic Health and Education Coverage', in Colclough, Christopher (ed.), *Marketizing Education and Health in Developing Countries: Miracle or Mirage?*. Oxford: Clarendon Press, pp.307-346.

Caillods, Françoise & Lewin, Keith (2001): 'Financing Increased Access and Participation at Secondary Level: Main Policy Options', in Lewin, Keith & Caillods, Françoise (eds.), *Financing Secondary Education in Developing Countries: Strategies for Sustainable Growth*. Paris: UNESCO International Institute for Educational Planning, pp.333-355.

Cambodia, Royal Government of (2002): *Cambodia Human Development Report*. Phnom Penh: Ministry of Planning in collaboration with United Nations Development Programme.

Chandler, David P. (1994): *A History of Cambodia*. Chiang Mai: Silkworm Books.

Chuor, Char Meng & Sereyrath, Sam (Co-Chairs) (2004): *Practices and Lessons Learned in the Management of Development Cooperation: Case Studies in Cambodia*. Government-Donor Partnership Working Group,

Sub-Working Group No.3. Phnom Penh: Council for the Development of Cambodia, and Cambodian Rehabilitation and Development Board.

Clayton, Thomas (1995): 'Restriction or Resistance? French Colonial Educational Development in Cambodia'. *Education Policy Analysis Archives*, Vol.3, No.19, pp.1-12.

Clayton, Thomas (2000): Review of Bray, Mark (1999) *The Private Costs of Public Schooling: Household and Community Financing of Primary Education in Cambodia*, in *Comparative Education*, Vol.30, No.3, pp.371-373.

Cohn, Elchanan & Geske, Terry G. (1990): *The Economics of Education*. third edition, New York: Pergamon Press.

Colclough, C., Rose, P. & Tembon, M. (2000): 'Gender Inequalities in Primary Schooling: The Roles of Poverty and Adverse Cultural Practice'. *International Journal of Educational Development*, Vol.20, No.1, pp.5-27.

Colclough, C., Al-Samarrai, S., Rose, P. & Tembon, M. (2003): *Achieving Schooling for All in Africa: Costs, Commitment and Gender*. Aldershot, UK: Ashgate.

Council for Social Development (2002): *National Poverty Reduction Strategy 2003-2005*. Phnom Penh: Council for Social Development.

Coyne, Geoffrey (2001): Review of Bray, Mark (1999) *The Private Costs of Public Schooling: Household and Community Financing of Primary Education in Cambodia*, in *Economics of Education Review*, Vol.20, No.3, pp.305-306.

Debande, Olivier (2004): 'A Review of Instruments for Student Loans in Tertiary Education'. *European Journal of Education*, Vol.39, No.2, pp.161-190.

Dy, Sideth S. (2004): 'Strategies and Policies for Basic Education in Cambodia: Historical Perspectives'. *International Education Journal*, Vol.5, No.1, pp.90-97.

Evans, Kiri & Rorris, Adam (1994): *Cost-Effectiveness of Primary Education in Myanmar*. Yangon: UNICEF.

Fair, Kristi K. (1998): 'The Demand for Education in Namibia: School Costs, Household Wealth, and Household Decision-Making Processes'. PhD dissertation, The Florida State University.

Foondun, A. Raffick (2002): 'The Issue of Private Tuition: An Analysis of the Practice in Mauritius and Selected South-East Asian Countries'. *International Review of Education*, Vol.48, No.6, pp.485-515.

Francis, Paul A. with Agi, S.P.I., Alubo, S.O., Biu, H.A., Daramola, A.G., Nzewi, U.M. & Shehu, D.J. (1998): *Hard Lessons: Primary Schools,*

Community, and Social Capital in Nigeria. Technical Paper No.420, Washington DC: The World Bank.

Geeves, R., Vanny, C., Pharin, K., Sereyrith, L., Heng, S. & Panhcharun, T. (2002): *Evaluation of the Impact of the Education Quality Improvement Project (EQIP) of the Ministry of Education, Youth and Sport of the Royal Government of Cambodia.* Phnom Penh: World Education Cambodia.

Glewwe, Paul (2000): 'Education', in Grosh, Margaret & Glewwe, Paul (eds.), *Designing Household Survey Questionnaires for Developing Countries: Lessons from 15 Years of Household Living Standards Measurement Study.* Vol.1, Washington DC: The World Bank, pp. 143-175.

Gourley, Steve (2000): *Look before you Lean: Strategic Approaches to Urban Child Labour.* Phnom Penh: World Vision Cambodia.

Hannum, Emily (2003): 'Poverty and Basic Education in China: Villages, Households, and Girls' and Boys' Enrolment'. *Comparative Education Review*, Vol.47, No.1, pp141-159.

Howes, Steven & Lanjouw, Jean Olson (1997): *Poverty Comparisons and Household Survey Design.* Living Standards Measurement Study (LSMS) Working Paper 129, Washington DC: The World Bank.

Ilon, Lynn & Moock, Peter (1991): 'School Attributes, Household Characteristics, and Demand for Schooling: A Case Study of Rural Peru'. *International Review of Education*, Vol.37, No.4, pp.429-451.

James, Estelle, King, Elizabeth M. & Suryadi, Ace (1996): 'Finance, Management, and Costs of Public and Private Schools in Indonesia'. *Economics of Education Review*, Vol.15, No.4, pp.387-398.

Jimenez, Emmanuel & Paqueo, Vicente (1996): 'Do Local Contributions Affect the Efficiency of Public Primary Schools?'. *Economics of Education Review*, Vol.15, No.4, pp.379-380.

Kadzamira, Esme & Rose, Pauline (2003): 'Can Free Primary Education Meet the Needs of the Poor? Evidence from Malawi'. *International Journal of Educational Development*, Vol.23, No.5, pp.501-516.

Kemmerer, Fran (1999): *Resources for Schooling: A Model for Local Accountability.* Project Preparatory Study No.1, Education Learning and Innovations Loan. Phnom Penh: Project Preparation Unit, Planning Department, Ministry of Education, Youth & Sport.

Keng, Chan Sopheak (2004a): 'Children Agency and Educational Expansion: The Cambodian Experience'. Paper presented at the 48th annual conference of the Comparative & International Education Society, Salt Lake City, USA, 9-12 March.

Keng, Chan Sopheak (2004b): 'Why do Girls Drop Out of School? Evidence from Rural Cambodia'. *The Journal of Cambodian Studies*, Vol.1, No.1, pp.5-16.

King, Elizabeth M. (1997): 'Who Really Pays for Education? The Roles of Government and Families in Indonesia', in Colclough, Christopher (ed.), *Marketizing Education and Health in Developing Countries: Miracle or Mirage?*. Oxford: Clarendon Press, pp.165-182.

Kwok, Percy (2004): 'Examination-Oriented Knowledge and Value Transformation in East Asian Cram Schools'. *Asia Pacific Education Review*, Vol.5, No.1, pp.64-75.

Lerotholi, Liteboho Maqalika (2001): *Tuition Fees in Primary and Secondary Education in Lesotho: The Levels and Implications for Access, Equity and Efficiency*. Paris: UNESCO International Institute for Educational Planning.

Manzon, Maria (2004): *Building Alliances: Schools, Parents and Communities in Hong Kong and Singapore*. Hong Kong: Comparative Education Research Centre, The University of Hong Kong.

Marchand, Jacques (2000): *Les Écoles Communautaires: Mali, Sénégal, Togo*. Paris: UNESCO International Institute for Educational Planning.

Marshall, Jeffery H. (2004): 'EQIP School Grants Program Evaluation: Final Report'. Phnom Penh: Education Quality Improvement Project, MoEYS.

McGinn, Noel F. & Welsh, Thomas (1999): *Decentralization of Education: Why, When, What and How*. Fundamentals of Educational Planning 64. Paris: UNESCO International Institute for Educational Planning.

McMahon, Walter W. (2002): *Education and Development: Measuring the Social Benefits*. New York: Oxford University Press.

Mehrotra, Santosh & Delamonica, Enrique (1998). 'Household Costs and Public Expenditure on Primary Education in Five Low-income Countries: A Comparative Analysis'. *International Journal of Educational Development*, Vol.18, No.1, pp.41-61.

Miller-Grandvaux, Yolande & Yoder, Karla (2002): *A Literature Review of Community Schools in Africa*. Washington DC: USAID Bureau for Africa, Office of Sustainable Development.

MoEYS [Ministry of Education, Youth & Sport] (2001a): *Priority Action Program for Improving the Quality and Effectiveness of Basic Education: Strategic Plan, Schedule of Activities and Budget Allocations*. Phnom Penh: MoEYS.

MoEYS [Ministry of Education, Youth & Sport] (2001b): Circular No.1820, July. Phnom Penh: MoEYS.

MoEYS [Ministry of Education, Youth & Sport] (2002a): *Education Sector Review Report – 2002*. Phnom Penh: MoEYS.

MoEYS [Ministry of Education, Youth & Sport] (2002b): 'Poverty Analysis of Education Access Trends: Discussion Paper. Phnom Penh: Mo-EYS.

MoEYS [Ministry of Education, Youth & Sport] (2002c): *Education Statistics and Indicators 2001/2002*. Phnom Penh: MoEYS.

MoEYS [Ministry of Education, Youth & Sport] (2003): *Education Sector Performance Report: ESSP Review 2003*. Phnom Penh: MoEYS.

MoEYS [Ministry of Education, Youth & Sport] (2004a): *Education Statistics and Indicators 2003/2004*. Phnom Penh: MoEYS.

MoEYS [Ministry of Education, Youth & Sport] (2004b): *Education Strategic Plan 2004/08*. Phnom Penh: MoEYS.

MoEYS [Ministry of Education, Youth & Sport] & KAPE [Kampuchean Action for Primary Education] (2001): 'Interim Report 1: Situation Analysis and Strategic Options. JFPR Appraisal and Project Design for Assistance to Poor Girls and Indigenous Children'. Phnom Penh: MoEYS & KAPE.

Mok, Ka Ho (ed.) (2003): *Centralization and Decentralization: Educational Reforms and Changing Governance in Chinese Societies*. Hong Kong: Comparative Education Research Centre, The University of Hong Kong.

Mukudi, Edith (2004): 'The Effects of User-Fee Policy on Attendance Rates Among Kenyan Schoolchildren'. *International Review of Education*, Vol.50, Nos.5-6, pp.447-461.

Mythili, N. (2000): Review of Bray, Mark (1999) *The Private Costs of Public Schooling: Household and Community Financing of Primary Education in Cambodia*, in *Perspectives in Education*, Vol.16, No.3, pp.195-199.

Naren, Kuch & Collins, Jennifer (2004): 'All Work, No Pay: Teachers in Three Provinces Deal with Low, Late Salaries'. *The Cambodia Daily*, 10-11 January, pp.4-5.

National EFA Assessment Group (1999): *Education for All (EFA): The Year 2000 Assessment – Country Report*. Phnom Penh: Ministry of Education, Youth & Sport.

National Education for All Commission (2003): *Education for All National Plan 2003-2005*. Phnom Penh: Secretariat of the National Education for All Commission.

National Institute of Statistics (2002): *Report on Cambodia Child Labour Survey 2001*. Phnom Penh: National Institute of Statistics, Ministry of Planning.

National Institute of Statistics (2004): 'National Consumer Price Index, Cambodia (Urban)'. Phnom Penh: National Institute of Statistics. www.nis. gov.kh/periodic/cpi/cpi.htm.

Obasi, Emma (2000): 'The Impact of Economic Recession on UPE in Nigeria'. *International Journal of Educational Development*, Vol.20, No.3, pp.189-207.

OECD [Organisation for Economic Co-operation & Development] & UNESCO [United Nations Educational, Scientific & Cultural Organisation] (2003): *Financing Education – Investments and Returns: Analysis of the World Education Indicators*. Paris: OECD and UNESCO.

Okuma-Nystrom, Michiyo Kiwako (2004): *God Turns the Chapter and Everything Changes: Children's Socialization in Two Gambian Villages*. Stockholm: Institute of International Education, Stockholm University.

Ondrusek, Robert (2002): 'Monitoring the Impact of Education Policy Reforms on the Poor'. Phnom Penh: UNICEF.

Penrose, Perran (1998): *Cost Sharing in Education: Public Finance, School and Household Perspectives*. London: Department for International Development.

Pheng, D., Savonn, H. & Soly, Y. (2001): *Educational Financing and Budgeting in Cambodia*. Paris: UNESCO International Institute for Educational Planning.

Patrinos, Harry A. (2002): Review of Bray, Mark (1999) *The Private Costs of Public Schooling: Household and Community Financing of Primary Education in Cambodia*, in *Education Economics*, Vol.10, No.1, pp.115-116

Psacharopoulos, George (2000): Review of Bray, Mark (1999) *The Private Costs of Public Schooling: Household and Community Financing of Primary Education in Cambodia*, in *International Journal of Educational Development*, Vol.20, No.5, pp.423-439.

Psacharopoulos, George & Patrinos, Harry Anthony (2004): 'Returns to Investment in Education: A Further Update'. *Education Economics*, Vol.12, No.2, pp.111-134.

Rose, Pauline (2003): 'Community Participation in School Policy and Practice in Malawi: Balancing Local Knowledge, National Policies and International Agency Priorities'. *Compare: A Journal of Comparative Education*, Vol.33, No.1, pp.47-64.

Rose, Pauline & Al-Samarrai, Samer (2001): 'Household Constraints on Schooling by Gender: Empirical Evidence from Ethiopia'. *Comparative Education Review*, Vol.45, No.1, pp.36-63.

Shimizu, Kazuki (1999): 'Thinking about the Country's Future from the Perspective of the Role of Traditional Organization: Primary School Construction Supported by Temples in Cambodia', in Kataoka, Sachihiko (ed.), *The Future of the Global Village*. Tokyo: Shinhyoron, pp.205-220. [in Japanese]

Sodhy, Pamela (2004): 'Modernization and Cambodia'. *Journal of Third World Studies*, Vol.XXI, No.1, pp.153-174.

Sokha, Pel & Seng, Suon (2000): *Household Economic Survey: Case Study in Three Villages – Prey Tayong, Prey Kes and Prey Rong, Kong Pesei District, Kampong Speu*. Phnom Penh: Centre d'Etude et de Développement Agricole Cambodgien at the request of the Japanese International Cooperation Agency.

Supriadi, Dedi (2003): *Satuan Biaya Pendidikan: Dasar dan Menengah [Unit Costs in Education: Primary and Secondary]*. Bandung: PT Remaja Rosdakarya.

Suzuki, Ikuko (2002a): 'The Notion of Participation in Primary Education in Uganda: Democracy in School Governance?', in Schweisfurth, M., Davies, L. & Harber, C. (eds.), *Learning Democracy and Citizenship: International Experiences*. Oxford: Symposium Books, pp.157-173.

Suzuki, Ikuko (2002b): 'Parental Participation and Accountability in Primary Schools in Uganda'. *Compare: A Journal of Comparative Education*, Vol.32, No.2, pp.243-259.

Swartland, J.R. & Taylor, D.C. (1988): 'Community Financing of Schools in Botswana', in Bray, Mark with Lillis, Kevin (eds.), *Community Financing of Education: Issues and Policy Implications in Less Developed Countries*. Oxford: Pergamon Press, pp.139-153.

Tan, Jason (1995): 'Joint Government-Malay Community Efforts to Improve Malay Educational Achievement in Singapore'. *Comparative Education*, Vol.31, No.3, pp.339-353.

Thompson, A.R. (1981): *Education and Development in Africa*. London: Macmillan.

Tilak, Jandhyala B.G. (1994a): *Education for Development in Asia*. New Delhi: Sage Publications.

Tilak, Jandhyala B.G. (1994b): *Financing Education in Cambodia*. Brisbane: Queensland Education Consortium for the Asian Development Bank.

Tilak, Jandhyala B.G. (1995): *How Free is 'Free' Education in India?*. Occasional Paper 21, New Delhi: National Institute of Educational Planning & Administration.

Tilak, Jandhyala B.G. (1997): 'Lessons from Cost Recovery in Education', in Colclough, Christopher (ed.), *Marketizing Education and Health in Developing Countries: Miracle or Mirage?*. Oxford: Clarendon Press, pp.63-89.

Tilak, Jandhyala B.G. (2003): 'Determinants of Household Expenditure on Education in India', in Tilak, Jandhyala B.G. (ed.), *Financing Education in India*. New Delhi: National Institute of Educational Planning & Administration, pp.284-308.

Tomasevski, Katarina (2003): *Education Denied: Cost and Remedies*. London: Zed Books.

Truong, T.K.C., Thai, T.N.D. & Bach, H.V. (1999): 'Educational Enrolments in Lower Secondary School', in Houghton, D., Haughton, J., Bales, S., Truong, T.K.C. & Nguyen, N.N. (eds.), *Health and Wealth in Vietnam: An Analysis of Household Living Standards*. Singapore: Institute of Southeast Asian Studies, pp.121-138.

Tsang, Mun C. (1997): 'Cost Analysis for Improved Policymaking and Evaluation'. *Educational Evaluation and Policy Analysis*, Vol.19, No.4, pp.318-324.

Turner, Mark (2002): 'Decentralization Facilitation: A Study of Decentralization in Cambodia with Specific Reference to Education'. Phnom Penh: Education Quality Improvement Project (EQIP), Ministry of Education, Youth & Sport.

UNESCO (2003): *EFA Global Monitoring Report 2003/4: Gender and Education for All – The Leap to Equality*. Paris: UNESCO.

United Nations Development Programme (1995): *Human Development Report 1995*. New York: Oxford University Press.

United Nations Development Programme (1997): *Cambodia Human Development Report 1997*. Phnom Penh: United Nations Development Programme.

United Nations Development Programme (2000): *Cambodia Human Development Report 2000: Children and Employment*. Phnom Penh: United Nations Development Programme.

United Nations Development Programme (2004): *Human Development Report 2004*. New York: Oxford University Press.

Urwick, James (2002): 'Determinants of the Private Costs of Primary and Early Childhood Education: Findings from Plateau State, Nigeria'. *In-

ternational Journal of Educational Development, Vol.22, No.2, pp.131-144.

Velasco, Esther (2001): 'Why are Girls Not in School? Perceptions, Realities and Contradictions in Changing Cambodia'. Phnom Penh: UNICEF.

Velasco, Esther (2004): 'Ensuring Gender Equity in Education for All: Is Cambodia on Track?'. *Prospects: Quarterly Review of Comparative Education*, Vol.XXXIV, No.1, pp.37-51.

Wang, Shanmai (2001): 'Cost Sharing Study: Gansu Basic Education Project (GBEP)'. Beijing: Center for Education & Economy Research, Beijing Normal University.

Watkins, Kevin (2000): *The Oxfam Education Report*. Oxford: Oxfam.

WCEFA [World Conference on Education for All] (1990a): *World Conference on Education for All: Final Report*. New York: Inter-Agency Commission, WCEFA.

WCEFA [World Conference on Education for All] (1990b): *World Declaration on Education for All*. New York: Inter-Agency Commission, WCEFA.

WEF [World Education Forum] (2000): *The Dakar Framework for Action – Education for All: Meeting our Collective Commitments*. Paris: UNESCO.

Woodhall, Maureen (2003): 'Student Loans in an International Context', in Guthrie, James W. (editor in chief), *Encyclopedia of Education*, second edition, Macmillan, New York, pp.2377-2381.

World Bank, The (1995): *Cambodia Rehabilitation Program: Implementation and Outlook*. Washington DC: The World Bank.

World Bank, The (1997): *World Development Report 1997: The State in a Changing World*. Washington DC: The World Bank.

World Bank, The (2000): *Bangladesh Education Sector Review*. Dhaka: The World Bank and University Press Ltd..

World Bank, The (2001): *A Chance to Learn: Knowledge and Finance for Education in Sub-Saharan Africa*. Washington DC: The World Bank.

World Bank, The (2003): *World Development Report 2004: Making Services Work for Poor People*. Washington DC: The World Bank.

World Bank, The (2004): *Cambodia: Quality Basic Education for All*. Washington DC: Human Development Unit (Education), East Asia & Pacific Region, The World Bank. [Draft]

World Bank & Asian Development Bank (2003): *Cambodia: Enhancing Service Delivery through Improved Resource Allocation and Institutional Reform – Integrated Fiduciary Assessment and Public Expendi-*

ture Review. Washington DC: The World Bank, and Manila: Asian Development Bank.

World Food Programme (2002): *Estimation of Poverty Rates at Commune-Level in Cambodia*. Phnom Penh: Ministry of Planning and World Food Programme.

Yoo, Yoon Ha (2002): *Economics of Private Tutoring: In Search for its Causes and Effective Cures*. Seoul: Korea Development Institute.

Zasloff, Joseph J. (2002): 'Emerging Stability in Cambodia'. *Asian Affairs*, Vol.28, No.4, pp.187-200.

Zhou, D., Mei, F. & Huang, P. (2003): 'Social Assessment Report of China Proposed Basic Education in Western Areas Project for Preparation of Ethnic Minority Education Strategy'. Report to the (UK) Department for International Development and the World Bank, Beijing.

Zoungrana, C.M., Tokindang, J., Marcoux, R. & Konate, M.K. (1997): *Family Dynamics and Education in an Urban Setting: A Study of Educational Inequalities between Boys and Girls in Bamako*. Abridged Research Report No.38, Nairobi: Academy Science Publishers.

Appendix Tables

Appendix Table 1: Household Expenditures on Primary Education, Phnom Penh, 2003/04 (Riels)

	Grade 1	Grade 2	Grade 3	Grade 4	Grade 5	Grade 6
School: Bak Touk (Urban) *Enrolment*	*909*	*933*	*1,079*	*1,140*	*1,107*	*1,167*
Registration expenses	300	300	3,100	300	300	2,800
Uniforms & equipment	24,190	24,190	25,650	26,200	27,460	32,100
Learning materials	10,540	13,450	15,070	20,020	21,540	25,240
Pocket money	70,560	71,820	71,820	73,080	88,200	100,800
Private tutoring	54,000	54,000	90,000	90,000	90,000	90,000
Tests & examinations	0	0	2,500	2,500	2,500	2,500
Transport	36,000	36,000	41,150	45,767	47,567	52,033
Other expenses	4,750	4,750	4,750	4,750	4,750	4,750
TOTAL	**200,340**	**204,510**	**254,040**	**262,617**	**282,317**	**310,223**

Appendix Table 2: Household Expenditures on Lower Secondary Education, Phnom Penh, 2003/04 (Riels)

	Grade 7	Grade 8	Grade 9
School: Bak Touk (Urban) *Enrolment*	*1,664*	*1,617*	*1,805*
Registration expenses	6,700	6,500	6,500
Uniforms & equipment	60,920	60,920	61,520
Learning materials	34,880	39,300	44,540
Pocket money	236,530	251,790	267,050
Private tutoring	118,083	118,083	412,020
Tests & examinations	40,000	40,000	44,000
Transport	80,267	80,267	80,267
Other expenses	3,000	3,000	3,000
TOTAL	**580,380**	**599,860**	**918,897**

Appendix Table 3: Household Expenditures on Primary Education, Kandal, 2003/04 (Riels)

	Grade 1	Grade 2	Grade 3	Grade 4	Grade 5	Grade 6
School: Prek Tmeiy (Semi-Urban)						
Enrolment	*217*	*244*	*247*	*222*	*214*	*185*
Registration expenses	0	0	200	2,500	200	2,200
Uniforms & equipment	15,870	16,770	17,130	20,900	21,500	22,640
Learning materials	6,320	7,510	8,530	10,690	12,570	15,090
Pocket money	35,280	40,320	46,620	51,660	56,700	59,220
Private tutoring	0	4,500	5,000	5,500	6,000	28,800
Tests & examinations	0	0	0	0	0	0
Transport	0	0	0	14,333	14,333	17,500
Other expenses	320	330	330	630	700	700
TOTAL	**57,790**	**69,430**	**77,810**	**106,213**	**112,003**	**146,150**
School: Prek Sdey (Rural)						
Registration expenses	0	0	200	700	200	1,900
Uniforms & equipment	13,340	14,620	15,880	15,830	17,420	17,860
Learning materials	3,850	4,850	7,280	8,230	10,630	13,130
Pocket money	23,940	27,720	30,240	42,840	42,840	45,360
Private tutoring	0	0	0	0	0	7,600
Tests & examinations	0	0	0	0	0	0
Transport	0	0	0	0	10,333	14,333
Other expenses	370	380	1,130	1,130	1,130	1,130
TOTAL	**41,500**	**47,570**	**54,730**	**68,730**	**82,553**	**101,313**

Appendix Table 4: Household Expenditures on Lower Secondary Education, Kandal, 2003/04 (Riels)

	Grade 7	Grade 8	Grade 9
School: Hun Sen Kor Thom (Semi-Urban) *Enrolment*	*294*	*259*	*176*
Registration expenses	2,500	500	500
Uniforms & equipment	46,230	46,230	46,730
Learning materials	20,260	25,590	31,480
Pocket money	152,600	160,230	167,860
Private tutoring	22,527	43,600	113,360
Tests & examinations	0	0	9,000
Transport	30,167	30,167	33,833
Other expenses	4,700	4,700	4,700
TOTAL	**278,983**	**311,017**	**407,463**
School: Prek Sdey (Rural)			
Enrolment	*479*	*309*	*255*
Registration expenses	2,200	700	700
Uniforms & equipment	31,080	34,720	34,720
Learning materials	16,000	17,700	19,600
Pocket money	105,280	109,900	152,600
Private tutoring	34,900	34,900	104,600
Tests & examinations	0	0	8,500
Transport	29,000	29,000	29,000
Other expenses	2,400	2,900	3,400
TOTAL	**220,860**	**229,820**	**353,120**

Appendix Table 5: Household Expenditures on Primary Education, Takeo, 2003/04 (Riels)

	Grade 1	Grade 2	Grade 3	Grade 4	Grade 5	Grade 6
School: Chambak (Semi-Urban) *Enrolment*	*134*	*142*	*190*	*141*	*161*	*127*
Registration expenses	300	300	300	2,600	300	300
Uniforms & equipment	14,560	14,560	14,560	17,760	17,760	17,760
Learning materials	4,730	6,150	10,620	13,120	13,210	14,110
Pocket money	40,320	40,320	40,320	44,100	57,960	60,480
Private tutoring	0	0	0	18,000	18,000	32,400
Tests & examinations	0	0	0	0	0	0
Transport	0	0	9,833	19,667	24,167	29,500
Other expenses	1,300	1,300	1,300	1,340	1,340	1,340
TOTAL	**61,210**	**62,630**	**76,933**	**116,587**	**132,737**	**155,890**
School: Chiso (Rural) *Enrolment*	*173*	*119*	*302*	*260*	*220*	*167*
Registration expenses	0	0	0	2,600	0	2,500
Uniforms & equipment	10,810	10,810	12,910	16,150	17,550	17,550
Learning materials	3,990	5,230	9,940	11,930	12,020	15,910
Pocket money	17,640	25,200	25,200	26,460	27,720	32,760
Private tutoring	0	0	0	0	180	2,880
Tests & examinations	0	0	0	0	0	0
Transport	0	0	8,333	20,333	25,000	28,667
Other expenses	300	300	300	300	300	300
TOTAL	**32,740**	**41,540**	**56,683**	**77,773**	**82,770**	**100,567**

Appendix Table 6: Household Expenditures on Lower Secondary Education, Takeo, 2003/04 (Riels)

	Grade 7	Grade 8	Grade 9
School: Bati (Semi-Urban) *Enrolment*	*553*	*442*	*569*
Registration expenses	3,100	1,600	1,600
Uniforms & equipment	44,040	44,040	44,040
Learning materials	20,610	26,260	31,740
Pocket money	80,878	88,508	96,138
Private tutoring	23,253	29,067	82,840
Tests & examinations	0	0	8,500
Transport	42,333	42,333	42,333
Other expenses	1,430	1,430	1,430
TOTAL	**215,645**	**233,238**	**308,621**
School: Chiso (Rural) *Enrolment*	*270*	*271*	*171*
Registration expenses	1,600	1,600	1,600
Uniforms & equipment	20,720	20,720	20,720
Learning materials	19,500	24,100	27,300
Pocket money	48,860	48,860	48,860
Private tutoring	0	0	48,000
Tests & examinations	0	0	8,000
Transport	36,800	36,800	36,800
Other expenses	1,000	1,000	1,000
TOTAL	**128,480**	**133,080**	**192,280**

Appendix Table 7: Household Expenditures on Primary Education, Kampot, 2003/04 (Riels)

	Grade 1	Grade 2	Grade 3	Grade 4	Grade 5	Grade 6
School: Sat Porng						
(Semi-Urban) *Enrolment*	106	139	141	155	166	118
Registration expenses	400	400	2,760	400	400	2,900
Uniforms & equipment	11,440	11,440	11,440	17,800	17,800	17,800
Learning materials	5,280	7,080	8,400	10,040	12,300	13,460
Pocket money	40,320	40,320	40,320	50,400	51,660	52,920
Private tutoring	0	0	18,720	28,800	36,000	43,200
Tests & examinations	200	300	400	600	800	1,000
Transport	0	0	9,833	19,667	24,167	29,500
Other expenses	530	530	530	530	530	530
TOTAL	**58,170**	**60,070**	**92,403**	**128,237**	**143,657**	**161,310**
School: Prey Kley						
(Rural) *Enrolment*	78	92	114	134	121	80
Registration expenses	0	0	0	2,300	0	3,000
Uniforms & equipment	11,440	11,440	11,440	15,560	15,560	15,560
Learning materials	5,520	7,480	9,000	10,840	13,300	14,660
Pocket money	25,200	25,200	25,200	36,540	40,320	44,100
Private tutoring	0	0	0	0	0	7,200
Tests & examinations	0	0	0	0	0	0
Transport	0	0	9,833	19,667	24,167	29,500
Other expenses	530	530	530	530	530	530
TOTAL	**42,690**	**44,650**	**56,003**	**85,437**	**93,877**	**114,550**

Appendix Table 8: Household Expenditures on Lower Secondary Education, Kampot, 2003/04 (Riels)

	Grade 7	Grade 8	Grade 9
School: Chhouk (Semi-Urban)			
Enrolment	702	530	450
Registration expenses	3,600	500	500
Uniforms & equipment	28,900	28,900	28,900
Learning materials	21,350	26,090	39,750
Pocket money	137,340	144,970	175,490
Private tutoring	54,500	104,640	191,840
Tests & examinations	11,000	11,000	19,500
Transport	32,000	32,000	32,000
Other expenses	1,500	1,500	1,500
TOTAL	**290,190**	**349,600**	**489,480**
School: Prey Kley (Rural)			
Enrolment	136	90	45
Registration expenses	2,800	300	300
Uniforms & equipment	22,120	22,120	22,120
Learning materials	21,200	22,700	35,900
Pocket money	73,220	76,300	79,380
Private tutoring	33,600	42,400	110,500
Tests & examinations	11,000	11,000	20,500
Transport	32,000	32,000	32,000
Other expenses	1,500	1,500	1,500
TOTAL	**197,440**	**208,320**	**302,200**

Appendix Table 9: Household Expenditures on Primary Education, Svay Rieng, 2003/04 (Riels)

	Grade 1	Grade 2	Grade 3	Grade 4	Grade 5	Grade 6
School: Sihanouk						
(Semi-Urban) *Enrolment*	*317*	*277*	*265*	*350*	*366*	*286*
Registration expenses	300	300	2,600	300	300	2,300
Uniforms & equipment	13,210	14,050	14,190	16,600	17,250	17,250
Learning materials	4,100	5,800	11,000	12,900	14,900	15,800
Pocket money	40,320	51,660	59,220	61,740	70,560	73,080
Private tutoring	36,000	36,000	32,400	37,800	43,200	64,800
Tests & examinations	0	0	0	0	0	0
Transport	0	0	17,667	21,500	26,500	30,333
Other expenses	220	220	2,000	2,800	3,580	3,880
TOTAL	**94,130**	**108,030**	**139,077**	**153,670**	**176,270**	**207,423**
School: Por Thom						
(Rural) *Enrolment*	*281*	*176*	*179*	*134*	*116*	*97*
Registration expenses	300	300	300	2,600	300	2,300
Uniforms & equipment	10,300	10,300	10,300	12,670	12,670	12,670
Learning materials	4,770	5,360	5,550	5,550	8,380	9,170
Pocket money	25,200	25,200	25,200	42,840	42,840	42,840
Private tutoring	0	0	0	0	0	0
Tests & examinations	0	0	0	0	0	0
Transport	0	0	0	12,333	17,333	17,333
Other expenses	100	100	100	200	200	200
TOTAL	**40,670**	**41,260**	**41,450**	**76,193**	**81,723**	**84,513**

Appendix Table 10: Household Expenditures on Lower Secondary Education, Svay Rieng, 2003/04 (Riels)

	Grade 7	Grade 8	Grade 9
School: Svay Rieng (Semi-Urban) *Enrolment*	*1,061*	*654*	*610*
Registration expenses	2,500	500	1,500
Uniforms & equipment	23,500	23,500	23,500
Learning materials	21,450	26,750	30,390
Pocket money	94,612	117,502	152,600
Private tutoring	39,240	39,240	117,720
Tests & examinations	0	0	5,800
Transport	35,333	35,333	35,333
Other expenses	5,160	5,160	5,160
TOTAL	**221,795**	**247,985**	**372,203**
School: Por Thom (Rural)			
Enrolment	*383*	*250*	*168*
Registration expenses	3,000	0	500
Uniforms & equipment	13,440	13,440	13,440
Learning materials	15,000	18,200	19,800
Pocket money	67,130	76,300	80,850
Private tutoring	0	0	17,400
Tests & examinations	3,200	3,200	6,700
Transport	30,700	30,700	30,700
Other expenses	1,400	1,400	1,400
TOTAL	**133,870**	**143,240**	**170,790**

Appendix Table 11: Household Expenditures on Primary Education, Battambang, 2003/04 (Riels)

	Grade 1	Grade 2	Grade 3	Grade 4	Grade 5	Grade 6
School: Au Dambang (Semi-Urban) *Enrolment*	*114*	*128*	*131*	*150*	*125*	*123*
Registration expenses	200	200	2,700	700	700	2,200
Uniforms & equipment	12,210	12,210	12,210	18,800	28,800	20,200
Learning materials	6,190	6,900	11,100	14,060	17,100	18,840
Pocket money	60,480	60,480	60,480	70,560	70,560	70,560
Private tutoring	0	0	0	7,800	17,040	20,160
Tests & examinations	0	0	0	0	0	0
Transport	0	0	16,500	26,667	31,333	36,000
Other expenses	200	200	220	300	320	300
TOTAL	**79,280**	**79,990**	**103,210**	**138,887**	**155,853**	**168,260**
School: Phoum Doung (Rural)						
Registration expenses	120	120	320	620	320	1,820
Uniforms & equipment	11,580	11,580	11,580	18,480	18,480	19,460
Learning materials	5,630	6,320	10,580	13,260	16,200	17,960
Pocket money	25,200	25,200	25,200	44,100	46,620	52,920
Private tutoring	0	0	0	0	0	0
Tests & examinations	0	0	0	0	0	0
Transport	0	0	14,500	19,333	23,333	27,333
Other expenses	200	200	220	300	300	300
TOTAL	**42,730**	**43,420**	**62,400**	**96,093**	**105,253**	**119,793**

Appendix Table 12: Household Expenditures on Lower Secondary Education, Battambang, 2003/04 (Riels)

	Grade 7	Grade 8	Grade 9
School: Au Dambang (Semi-Urban) *Enrolment*	*355*	*266*	*252*
Registration expenses	3,600	600	600
Uniforms & equipment	27,250	27,250	27,250
Learning materials	26,200	28,410	30,620
Pocket money	149,548	149,548	166,334
Private tutoring	20,280	53,640	130,800
Tests & examinations	0	0	6,000
Transport	38,000	38,000	38,000
Other expenses	1,000	1,000	1,000
TOTAL	**265,878**	**298,448**	**400,604**
School: Banan (Rural) *Enrolment*	*336*	*216*	*111*
Registration expenses	3,100	600	600
Uniforms & equipment	16,870	16,870	16,870
Learning materials	20,400	21,500	26,900
Pocket money	122,080	129,710	152,600
Private tutoring	4,800	9,000	57,800
Tests & examinations	0	0	6,000
Transport	42,700	42,700	42,700
Other expenses	1,500	1,500	1,500
TOTAL	**211,450**	**221,880**	**304,970**

Appendix Table 13: Household Expenditures on Primary Education, Banteay Meanchey, 2003/04 (Riels)

	Grade 1	Grade 2	Grade 3	Grade 4	Grade 5	Grade 6
School: Au Ambel (Semi-Urban) *Enrolment*	*221*	*240*	*247*	*242*	*233*	*208*
Registration expenses	0	0	4,000	500	500	3,000
Uniforms & equipment	14,730	14,730	14,730	20,460	20,460	20,880
Learning materials	8,660	11,060	13,050	15,840	17,620	21,440
Pocket money	60,480	60,480	60,480	70,560	73,080	79,380
Private tutoring	18,000	18,000	18,000	18,000	18,000	32,400
Tests & examinations	0	0	0	0	0	0
Transport	0	0	0	5,500	13,333	22,000
Other expenses	1,400	1,400	1,400	1,500	1,500	6,100
TOTAL	**103,270**	**105,670**	**111,660**	**132,360**	**144,493**	**185,200**
School: Rohatek (Rural) *Enrolment*	*90*	*137*	*149*	*177*	*144*	*140*
Registration expenses	200	200	500	200	200	2,700
Uniforms & equipment	10,810	10,810	10,810	16,380	16,380	16,380
Learning materials	7,710	9,360	10,230	12,140	12,560	14,650
Pocket money	40,320	40,320	40,320	64,260	64,260	64,260
Private tutoring	0	0	0	0	0	0
Tests & examinations	0	0	0	0	0	0
Transport	0	0	0	13,667	19,333	27,333
Other expenses	700	750	950	1,900	1,900	1,900
TOTAL	**59,740**	**61,440**	**62,810**	**108,547**	**114,633**	**127,223**

Appendix Table 14: Household Expenditures on Lower Secondary Education, Banteay Meanchey, 2003/04 (Riels)

	Grade 7	Grade 8	Grade 9
School: Krom Phreas Norodom Ranarith (Semi-Urban) *Enrolment*	*957*	*628*	*551*
Registration expenses	4,500	1,500	1,500
Uniforms & equipment	34,380	34,380	34,380
Learning materials	25,090	28,450	35,850
Pocket money	152,600	152,600	152,600
Private tutoring	88,860	88,860	226,960
Tests & examinations	11,000	11,000	17,000
Transport	46,000	46,000	46,000
Other expenses	10,200	10,200	10,200
TOTAL	**372,630**	**372,990**	**524,490**
School: Rohatek (Rural) *Enrolment*	*230*	*159*	*142*
Registration expenses	4,300	1,300	1,300
Uniforms & equipment	18,060	18,060	18,060
Learning materials	15,300	17,700	24,200
Pocket money	137,340	152,600	160,230
Private tutoring	13,500	13,500	23,100
Tests & examinations	3,000	3,000	9,000
Transport	46,000	46,000	+
Other expenses	3,700	3,700	3,700
TOTAL	**241,200**	**255,860**	**285,590**

Appendix Table 15: Household Expenditures on Primary Education, Ratanakiri, 2003/04 (Riels)

	Grade 1	Grade 2	Grade 3	Grade 4	Grade 5	Grade 6
School: Phoum Tmeiy (Urban) *Enrolment*	*154*	*103*	*100*	*66*	*81*	*57*
Registration expenses	0	0	0	3,000	0	3,000
Uniforms & equipment	14,040	14,720	16,600	17,680	22,300	24,180
Learning materials	6,900	7,800	7,890	11,040	13,380	14,240
Pocket money	68,040	73,080	73,080	90,720	94,500	100,800
Private tutoring	0	0	0	16,200	21,600	21,600
Tests & examinations	0	0	0	0	0	0
Transport	0	0	16,967	17,267	18,233	18,233
Other expenses	500	500	500	900	1,600	1,700
TOTAL	**89,480**	**96,100**	**115,037**	**156,807**	**171,613**	**183,753**
School: Sangkom Meanchey (Rural) *Enrolment*	*284*	*51*	*36*	*31*	*39*	*27*
Registration expenses	0	0	0	1,500	0	2,500
Uniforms & equipment	14,385	14,880	15,010	18,230	18,405	21,450
Learning materials	5,970	7,100	8,670	9,870	11,150	12,150
Pocket money	22,680	22,680	23,940	31,500	42,840	46,620
Private tutoring	0	0	0	0	0	0
Tests & examinations	0	0	0	0	0	0
Transport	0	0	7,042	8,833	10,875	14,083
Other expenses	200	200	200	200	900	1,400
TOTAL	**43,235**	**44,860**	**54,862**	**70,133**	**84,170**	**98,203**

Appendix Table 16: Household Expenditures on Lower Secondary Education, Ratanikiri, 2003/04 (Riels)

	Grade 7	Grade 8	Grade 9
School: Samdach Ouv Samdach Mer (Urban) *Enrolment*	*161*	*175*	*250*
Registration expenses	4,000	1,000	1,000
Uniforms & equipment	43,870	44,710	44,710
Learning materials	20,720	21,620	24,900
Pocket money	144,970	144,970	144,970
Private tutoring	107,000	144,500	315,400
Tests & examinations	12,500	12,500	22,000
Transport	21,000	24,667	24,667
Other expenses	5,000	5,000	5,000
TOTAL	**359,060**	**398,967**	**582,647**

Notes on the Authors

Mark Bray is Dean of the Faculty of Education and Chair Professor of Comparative Education at the University of Hong Kong. He is also President of the World Council of Comparative Education Societies (WCCES). Among his specialisms is the economics and financing of education. He has conducted consultancy assignments in over 50 countries for such bodies as the Asian Development Bank, British Council, Commonwealth Secretariat, UNDP, UNESCO, UNICEF and the World Bank. He has also published extensively in the fields of educational planning and comparative education. *Address*: Comparative Education Research Centre, Faculty of Education, The University of Hong Kong, Pokfulam Road, Hong Kong, China. E-mail: mbray@hku. hk.

Seng Bunly is the director of BN Consult in Phnom Penh, Cambodia. He originally trained in the medical profession, before turning to work in the social sector. He holds an MSc in financial economics from the School of Oriental & African Studies at the University of London, and has considerable experience of consultancy projects funded by both national and international bodies. This includes membership of the team for Cambodia's National Poverty Reduction Strategy; and he has been the local analyst in Cambodia for the Program Impact Assessment of the United Nations Capital Development Fund. *Address*: BN Consult, No. 62, 111 Street, Phnom Penh, Cambodia. E-mail: sengbunly@bnckh. com.

Index

CERC Publications

Series: CERC Monographs

1. Yoko Yamato (2003): *Education in the Market Place: Hong Kong's International Schools and their Mode of Operation.* ISBN 962-8093-57-6. 117pp. HK$100/US$16.

2. Mark Bray, Ding Xiaohao & Huang Ping (2004): *Reducing the Burden on the Poor: Household Costs of Basic Education in Gansu, China.* ISBN 962-8093-32-0. 67pp. HK$50/US$10. [Also available in Chinese]

3. Maria Manzon (2004): *Building Alliances: Schools, Parents and Communities in Hong Kong and Singapore.* ISBN 962-8093-36-3. 117pp. HK$100/US$16.

4. Mark Bray & Seng Bunly (2005): *Balancing the Books: Household Financing of Basic Education in Cambodia.* ISBN 962-8093-39-8. 113pp. HK$100/US$16.

Series: Education in Developing Asia

1. Don Adams (2004): *Education and National Development: Priorities, Policies, and Planning.* ISBN 971-561-529-5. 81pp. HK$100/US$12 each or HK$400/US$50 for set of five.

2. David Chapman (2004): *Management and Efficiency in Education: Goals and Strategies.* ISBN 971-561-530-9. 85pp. HK$100/US$12 each or HK$400/US$50 for set of five.

3. Mark Bray (2004): *The Costs and Financing of Education: Trends and Policy Implications.* ISBN 971-561-531-7. 78pp. HK$100/US$12 each or HK$400/US$50 for set of five.

4. W.O. Lee (2004): *Equity and Access to Education: Themes, Tensions, and Policies.* ISBN 971-561-532-5. 101pp. HK$100/US$12 each or HK$400/US$50 for set of five.

5. David Chapman & Don Adams (2004): *The Quality of Education: Dimensions and Strategies.* ISBN 971-561-533-3. 72pp. HK$100/US$12 each or HK$400/US$50 for set of five.

Series: CERC Studies in Comparative Education

1. Mark Bray & W.O. Lee (eds.) (2001): *Education and Political Transition: Themes and Experiences in East Asia.* Second edition. ISBN 962-8093-84-3. 228pp. HK$200/US$32.

2. Mark Bray & W.O. Lee (eds.) (1997): *Education and Political Transition: Implications of Hong Kong's Change of Sovereignty.* ISBN 962-8093-90-8. 169pp. [Out of print]

3. Philip G. Altbach (1998): *Comparative Higher Education: Knowledge, the University, and Development.* ISBN 962-8093-88-6. 312pp. HK$180/US$30.

4. Zhang Weiyuan (1998): *Young People and Careers: A Comparative Study of Careers Guidance in Hong Kong, Shanghai and Edinburgh.* ISBN 962-8093-89-4. 160pp. HK$180/US$30.

5. Harold Noah & Max A. Eckstein (1998): *Doing Comparative Education: Three Decades of Collaboration.* ISBN 962-8093-87-8. 356pp. HK$250/US$38.

6. T. Neville Postlethwaite (1999): *International Studies of Educational Achievement: Methodological Issues.* ISBN 962-8093-86-X. 86pp. HK$100/US$20.

7. Mark Bray & Ramsey Koo (eds.) (2004): *Education and Society in Hong Kong and Macao: Comparative Perspectives on Continuity and Change.* Second edition. ISBN 962-8093-34-7. 323pp. HK$200/US$32.

8. Thomas Clayton (2000): *Education and the Politics of Language: Hegemony and Pragmatism in Cambodia, 1979-1989.* ISBN 962-8093-83-5. 243pp. HK$200/US$32.

9. Gu Mingyuan (2001): *Education in China and Abroad: Perspectives from a Lifetime in Comparative Education.* ISBN 962-8093-70-3. 260pp. HK$200/US$32.

10. William K. Cummings, Maria Teresa Tatto & John Hawkins (eds.) (2001): *Values Education for Dynamic Societies: Individualism or Collectivism.* ISBN 962-8093-71-1. 312pp. HK$200/US$32.

11. Ruth Hayhoe & Julia Pan (eds.) (2001): *Knowledge Across Cultures: A Contribution to Dialogue Among Civilizations.* ISBN 962-8093-73-8. 391pp. HK$250/US$38.

12. Robert A. LeVine (2003): *Childhood Socialization: Comparative Studies of Parenting, Learning and Educational Change.* ISBN 962-8093-61-4. 299pp. HK$200/US$32.

13. Mok Ka-Ho (ed.) (2003): *Centralization and Decentralization: Educational Reforms and Changing Governance in Chinese Societies.* ISBN 962-8093-58-4. 230pp. HK$200/US$32.

14. W.O. Lee, David L. Grossman, Kerry J. Kennedy & Gregory P. Fairbrother (eds.) (2004): *Citizenship Education in Asia and the Pacific: Concepts and Issues.* ISBN 962-8093-59-2. 313pp. HK$200/US$32.

15. Alan Rogers (2004): *Non-formal Education: Flexible Schooling or Participatory Education?.* ISBN 962-8093-30-4. 306pp. HK$200/US$32.

16. Peter Ninnes & Meeri Hellstén (eds.) (2005): *Internationalizing Higher Education: Critical Explorations of Pedagogy and Policy.* ISBN 962-8093-37-1. 231pp. HK$200/US$32.

Other books published by CERC

1. Mark Bray & R. Murray Thomas (eds.) (1998): *Financing of Education in Indonesia*. ISBN 971-561-172-9. 133pp. HK$140/US$20.

2. David A. Watkins & John B. Biggs (eds.) (1996, reprinted 1999): *The Chinese Learner: Cultural, Psychological and Contextual Influences*. ISBN 0-86431-182-6. 285pp. HK$200/US$32.

3. Ruth Hayhoe (1999): *China's Universities 1895-1995: A Century of Cultural Conflict*. ISBN 962-8093-81-9. 299pp. HK$200/US$32.

4. David A. Watkins & John B. Biggs (eds.) (2001): *Teaching the Chinese Learner: Psychological and Pedagogical Perspectives*. ISBN 962-8093-72-X. 306pp. HK$200/US$32.

5. 貝磊、古鼎儀編 (2002)。《香港與澳門的教育與社會：從比較角度看延續與變化》。ISBN 962-8093-94-9. 250pp. HK$200/US$32.

6. Mark Bray with Roy Butler, Philip Hui, Ora Kwo & Emily Mang (2002): *Higher Education in Macau: Growth and Strategic Development*. ISBN 962-8093-60-6. 127pp. HK$150/US$24.

7. Yoko Yamato & Sally Course (2002): *Guide to International Schools in Hong Kong*. ISBN 962-8093-62-2. 82pp. HK$72/US$12.

8. Ruth Hayhoe (2004): *Full Circle: A Life with Hong Kong and China*. ISBN 962-8093-31-2. 261pp. HK$200/US$32.

9. 贝磊、丁小浩、黄平 (2004):《减轻贫困家庭的负担: 中国甘肃基础教育的家庭成本》。ISBN 962-8093-33-9。53pp。HK$50/US$10 [Also available in English]

Order through bookstores or from:

Comparative Education Research Centre
Faculty of Education
The University of Hong Kong
Pokfulam Road
Hong Kong, China.

Fax: (852) 2517 4737
E-mail: cerc@hkusub.hku.hk
Website: www.hku.hk/cerc

The list prices above are applicable for order from CERC, and include sea mail postage; add US$5 per copy for air mail.